Welcome to the colorful adventure! Grab your crayons and get ready to embark on an exciting journey through the animal kingdom! Each page invites you to meet a new animal on a unique adventure.

To make it easier for you to find your favorite friends, we've organized the drawings in alphabetical order. This way, you can quickly find the brave lion, the striped zebra, and the wise turtle.

Get your crayons, markers, and pens ready, and let your creativity run wild! Each page is a new invitation to have fun and learn while coloring the most amazing animals in nature.

Explore, play, and learn with every page!

1. ☐ Antelope
2. ☐ Antelope Sable
3. ☐ Bear
4. ☐ Beaver
5. ☐ Buffalo
6. ☐ Butterfly
7. ☐ Camel
8. ☐ Chameleon
9. ☐ Cheetah
10. ☐ Chimpanzee
11. ☐ Crocodile
12. ☐ Deer
13. ☐ Dolphin
14. ☐ Duck
15. ☐ Eagle
16. ☐ Elephant
17. ☐ Fox
18. ☐ Frog
19. ☐ Giraffe
20. ☐ Hamster
21. ☐ Hippopotamus
22. ☐ Horse
23. ☐ Hyena
24. ☐ Hummingbird
25. ☐ Iguana
26. ☐ Jaguar
27. ☐ Kangaroo

28. ☐ Koala
29. ☐ Lion
30. ☐ Llama
31. ☐ Monkey
32. ☐ Owl
33. ☐ Octopus
34. ☐ Ostrich
35. ☐ Otter
36. ☐ Panda bear
37. ☐ Panther
38. ☐ Parrot
39. ☐ Peacock
40. ☐ Penguin
41. ☐ Puma
42. ☐ Rabbit
43. ☐ Raccoon
44. ☐ Rhino
45. ☐ Seahorse
46. ☐ Shark
47. ☐ Snail
48. ☐ Tiger
49. ☐ Toucan
50. ☐ Turtle
51. ☐ Walrus
52. ☐ Wolf
53. ☐ Zebra

Coloring the Animal Kingdom:

Author: Bartolomeu Jorge

Copyright:© 2024 Bartolomeu Jorge

All rights reserved.

No part of this book may be reproduced, stored in a retrieval system, or transmitted, in any form or by any means, electronic, mechanical, photocopying, recording, or otherwise, without the prior written permission of the author.

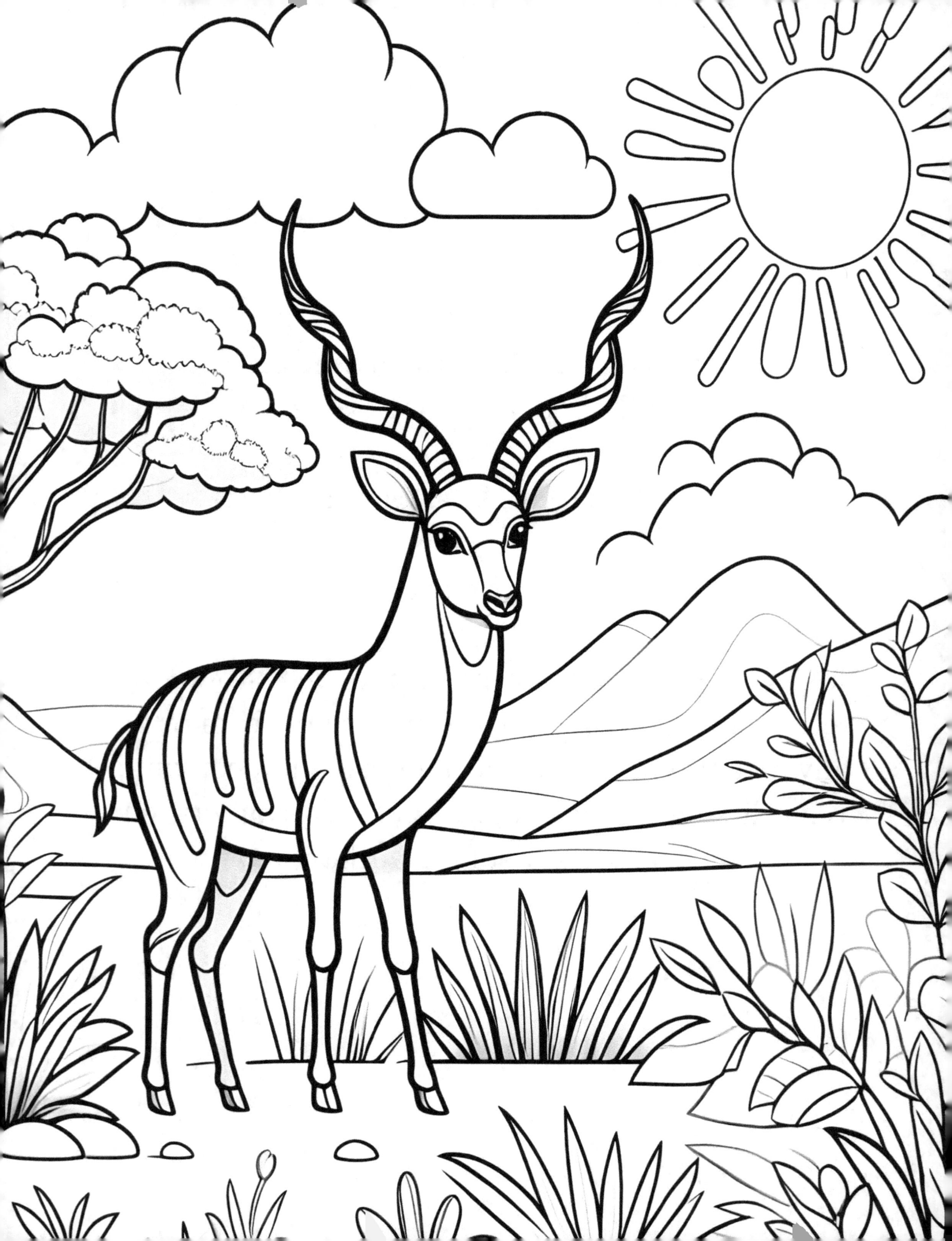

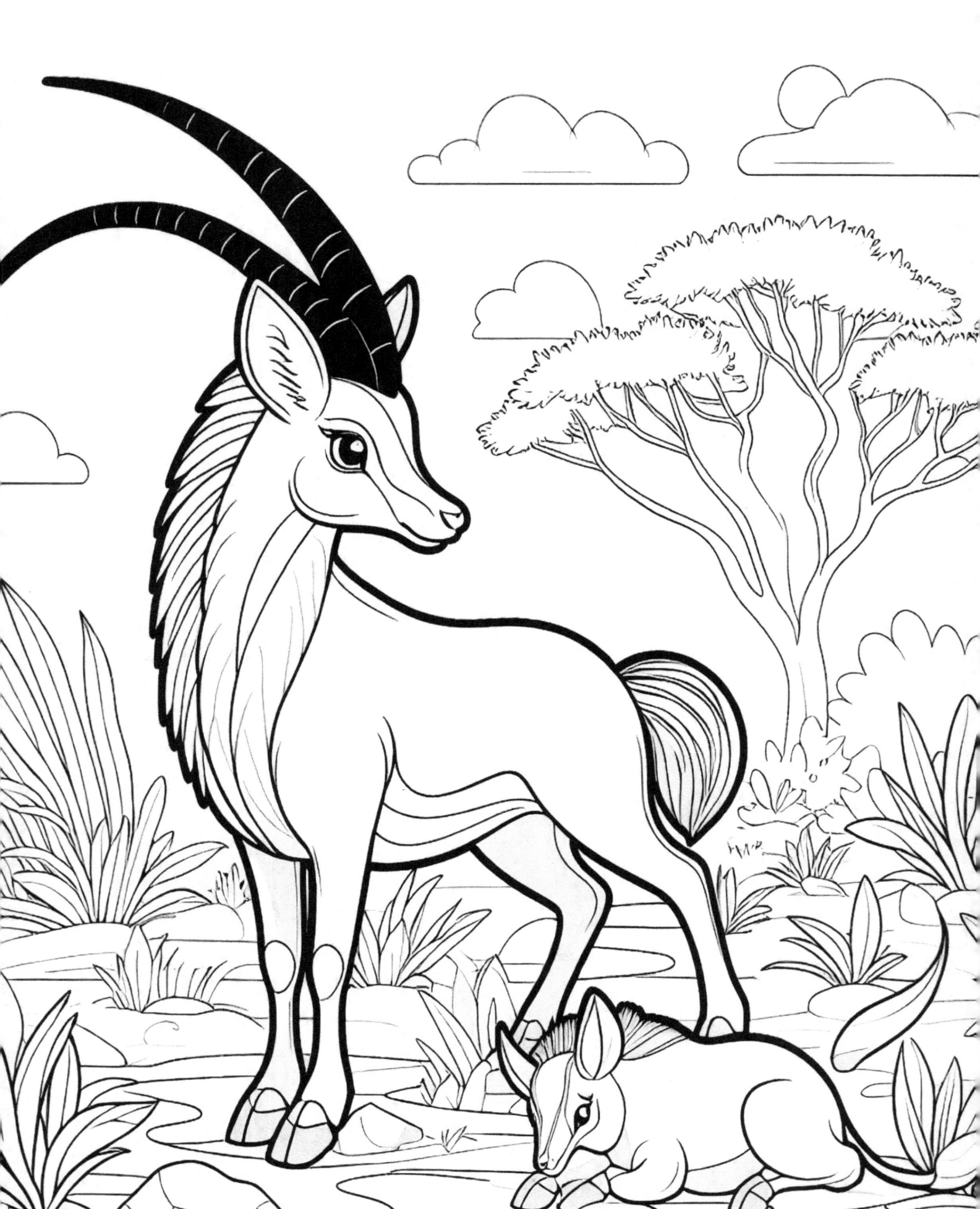

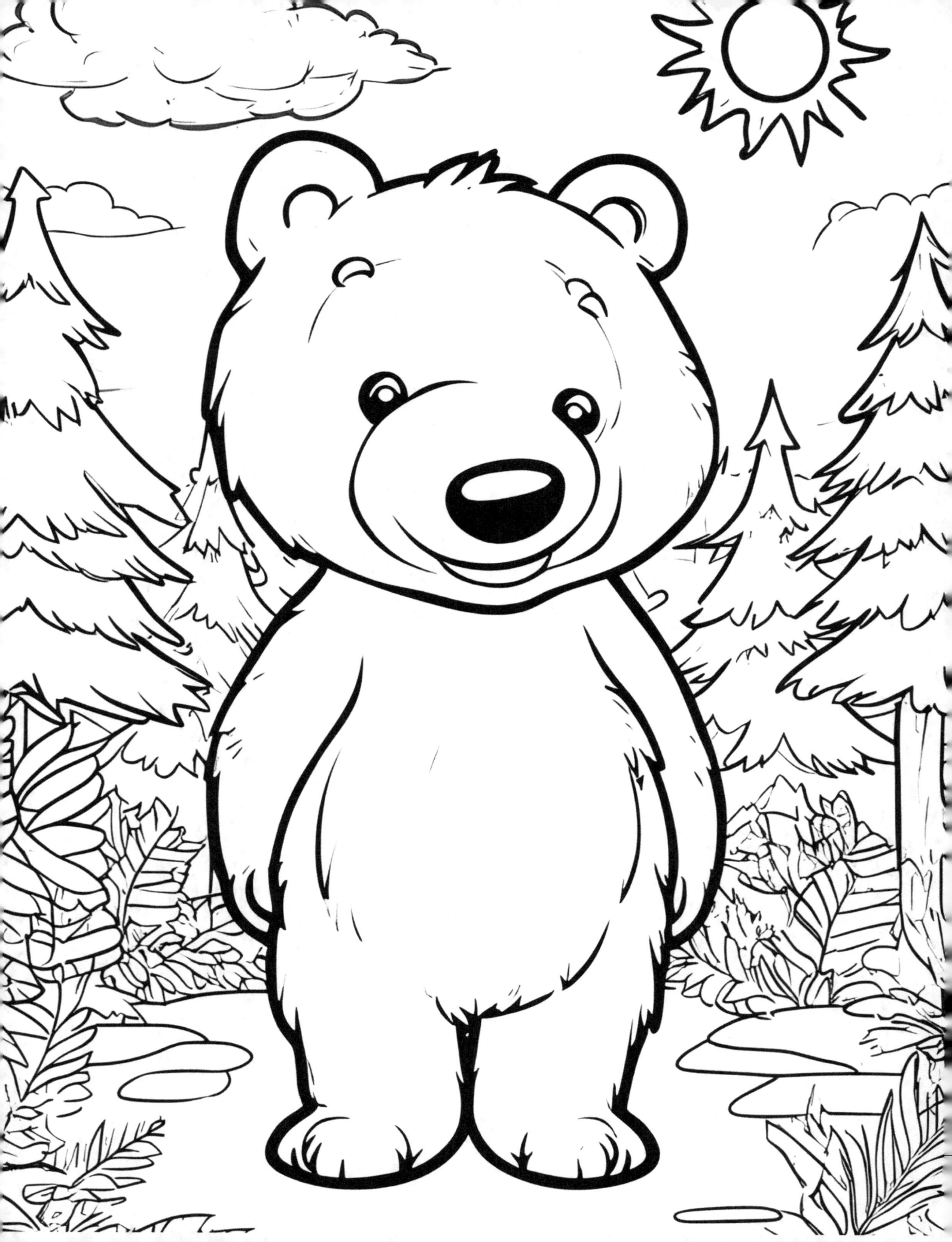

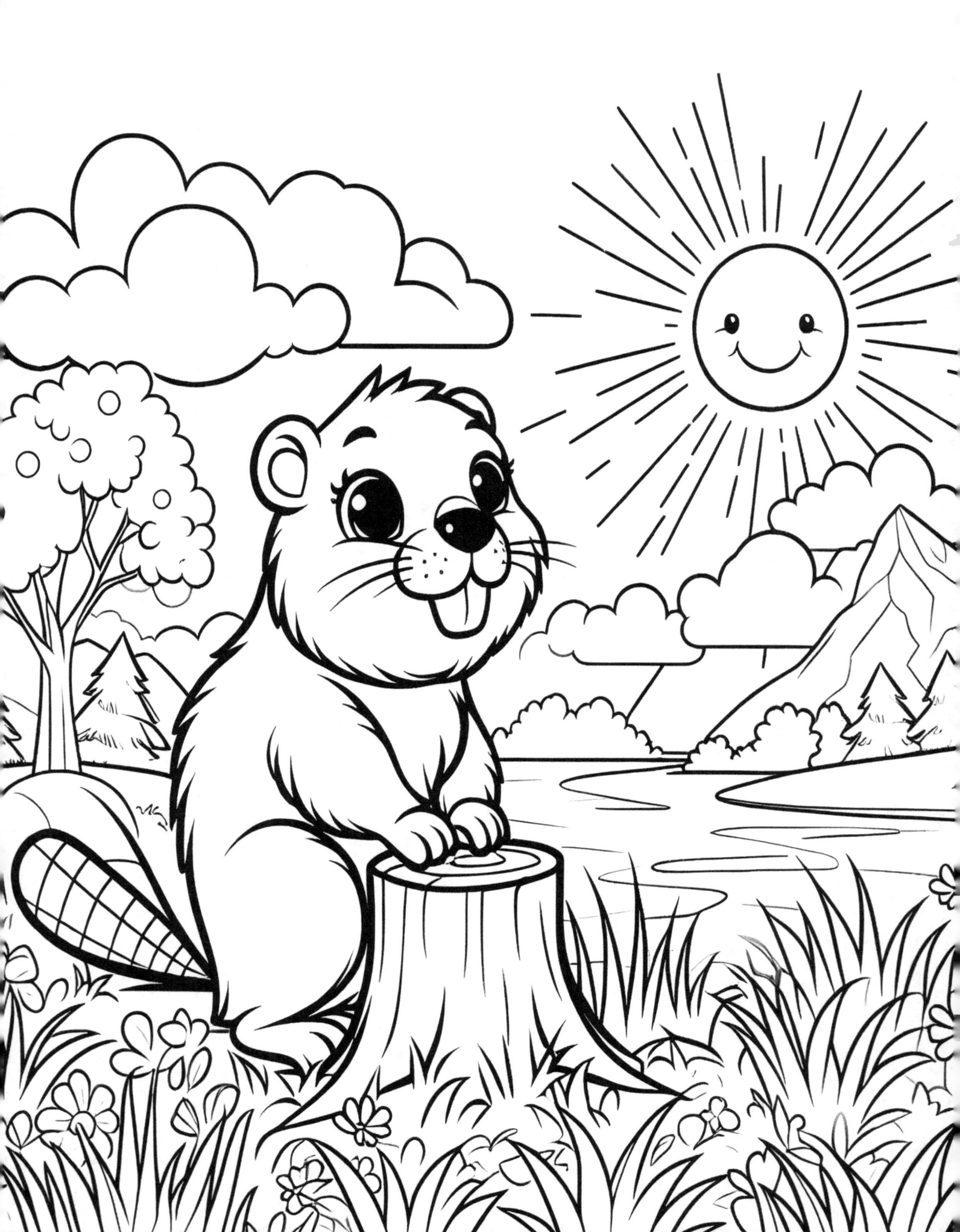

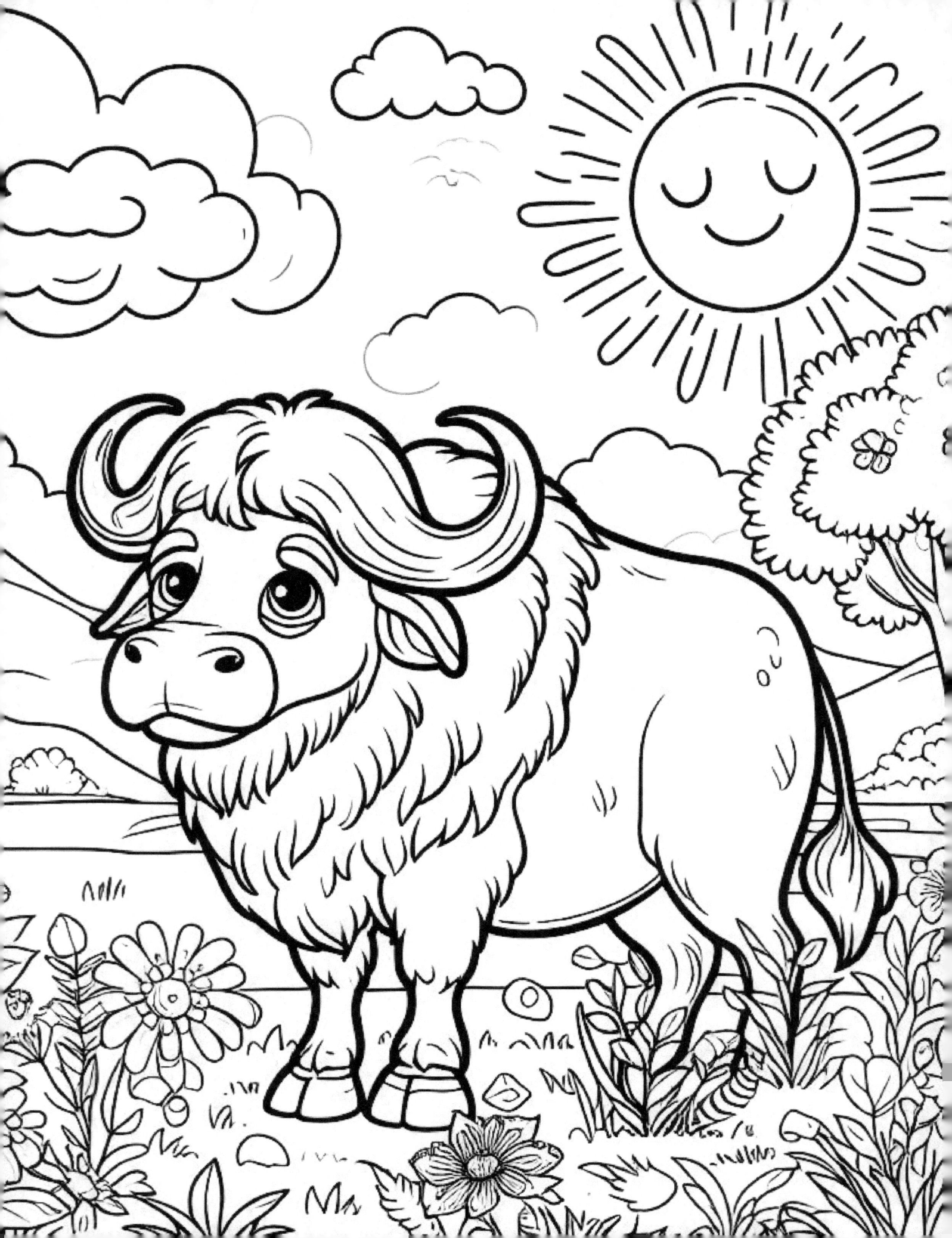

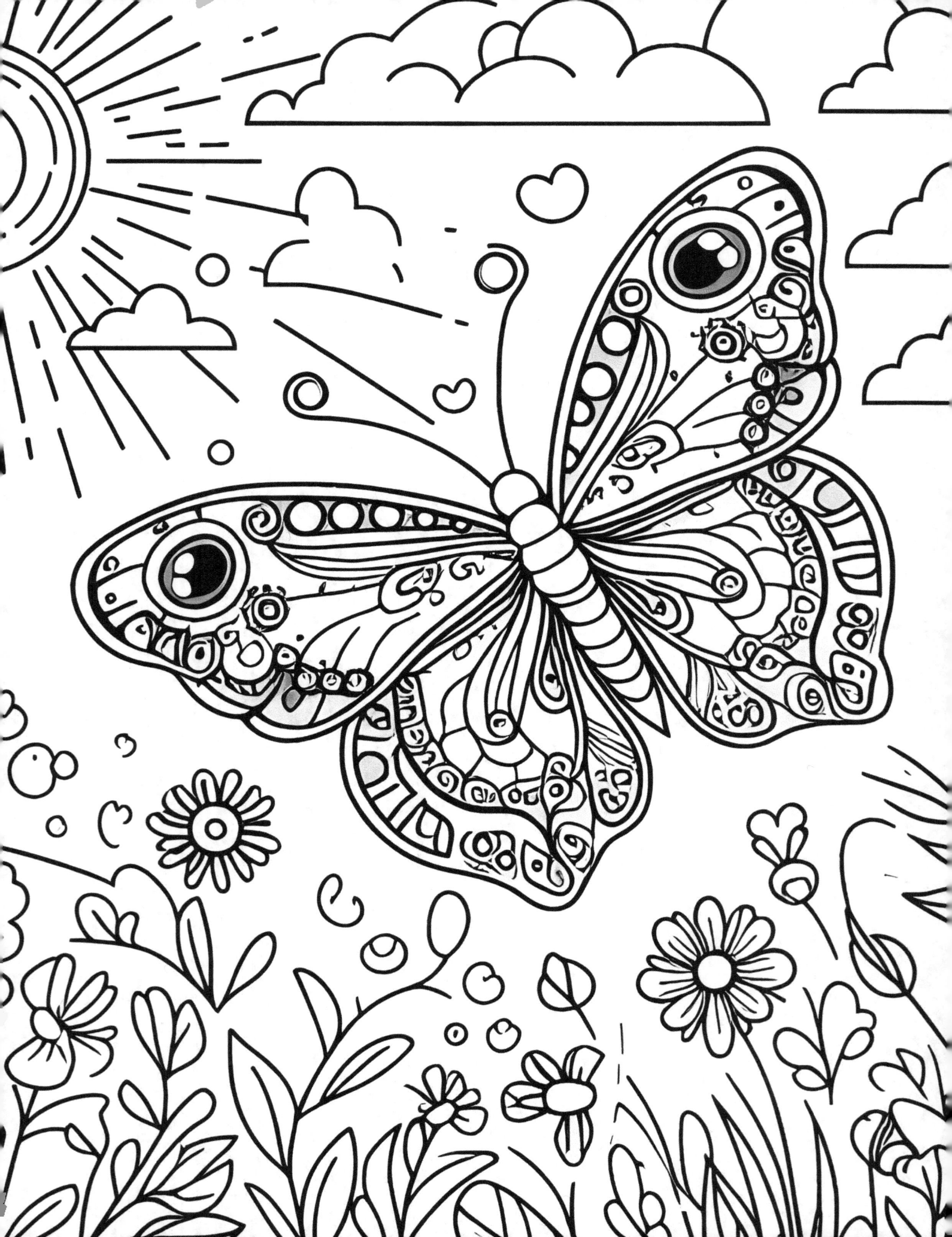

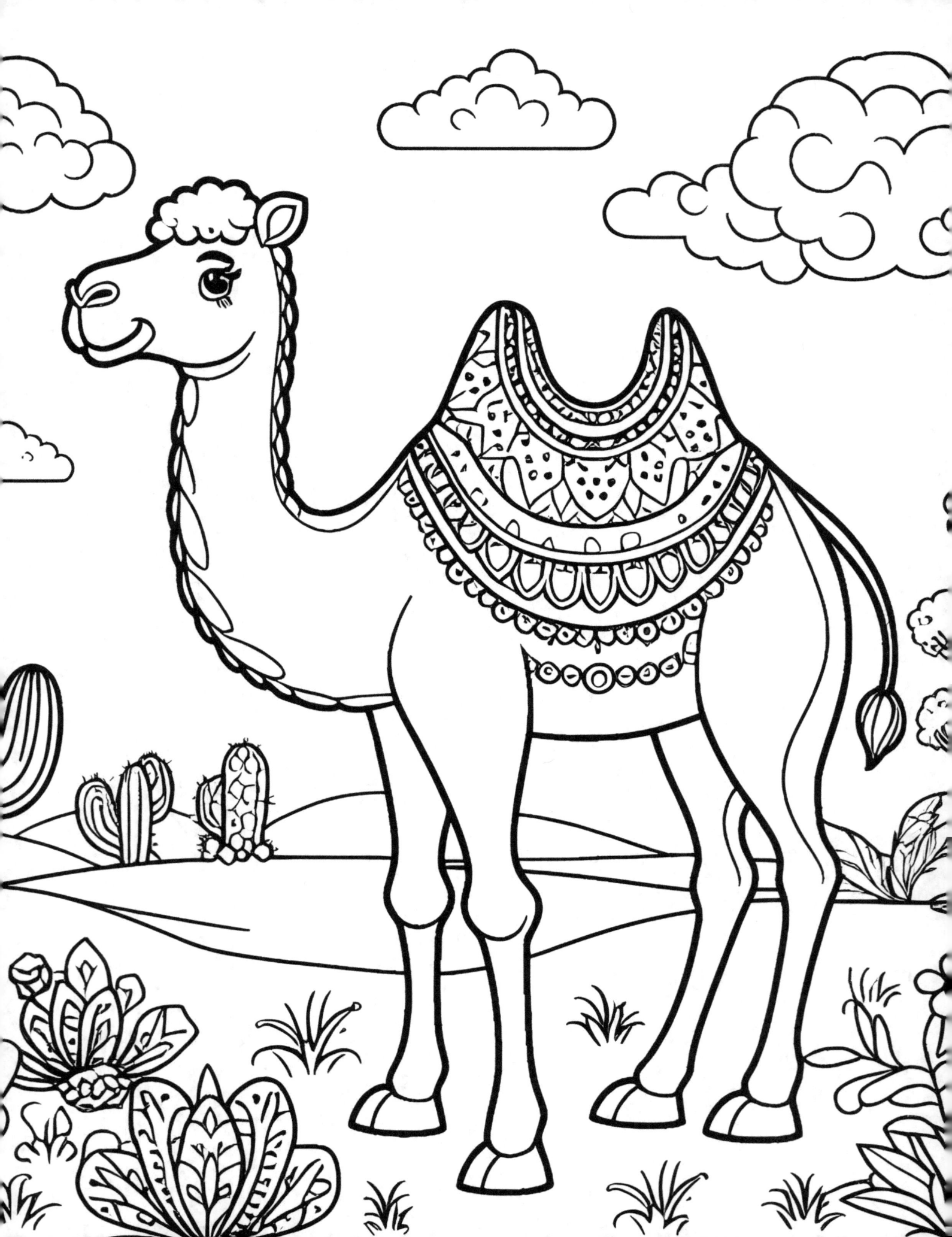

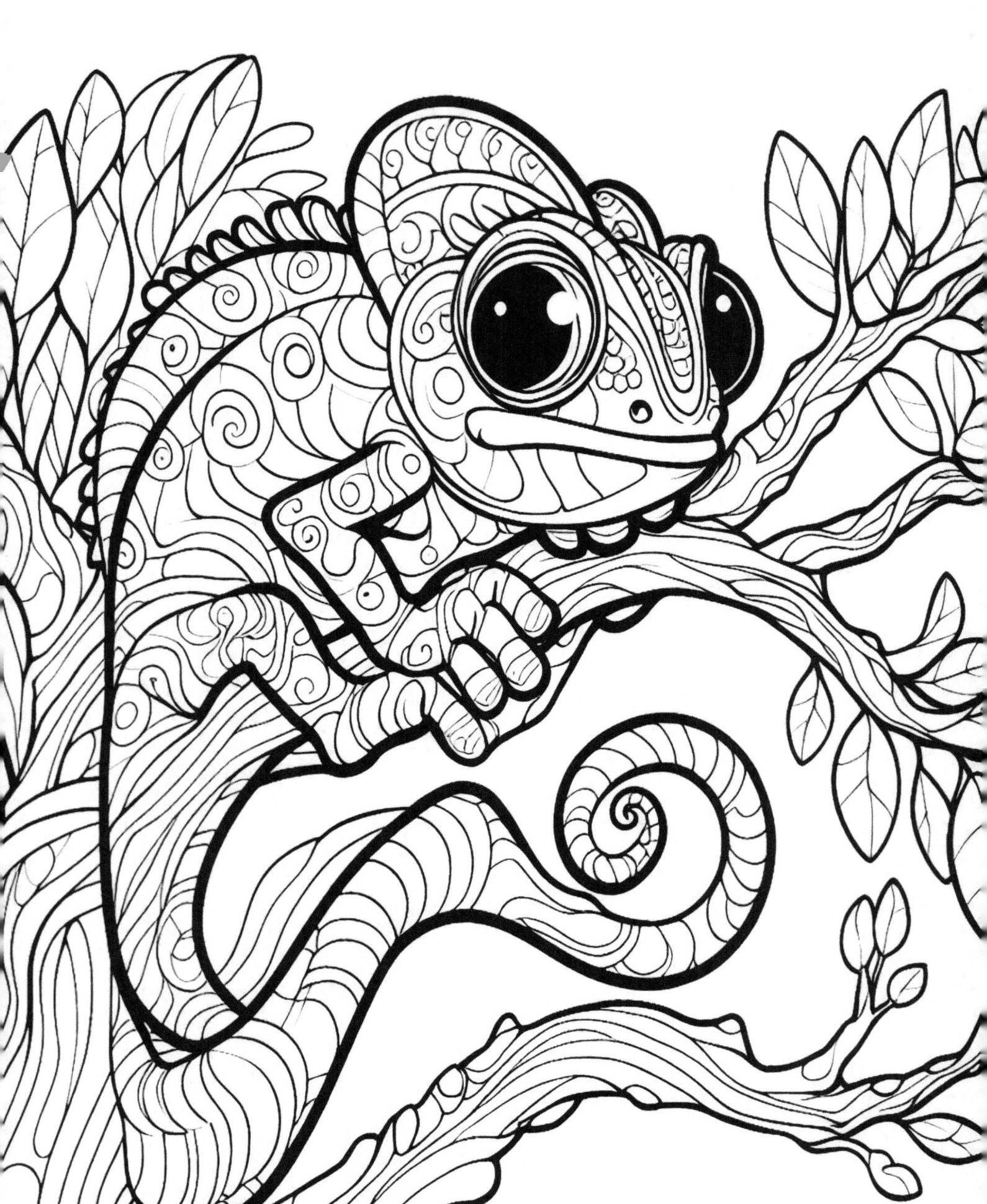

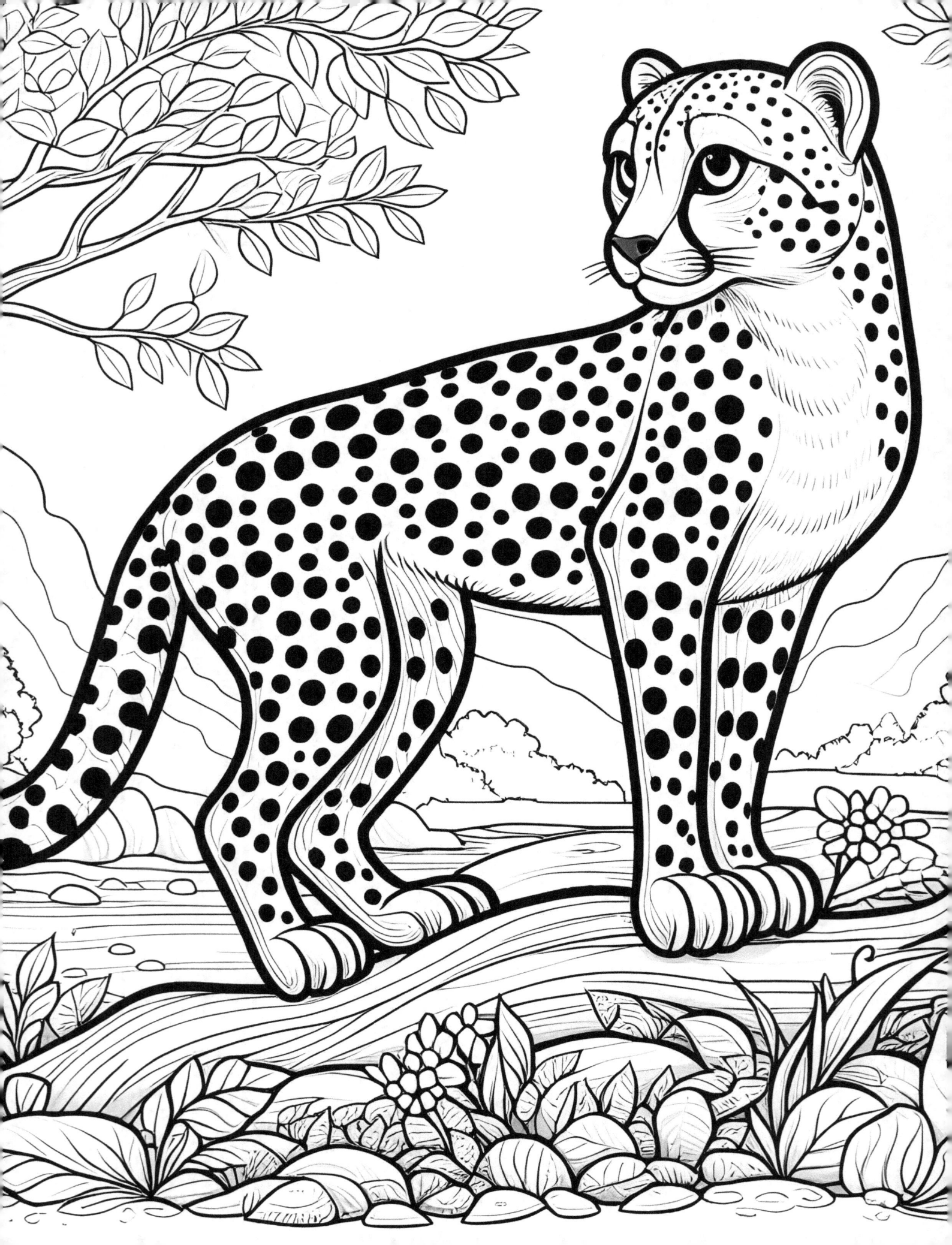

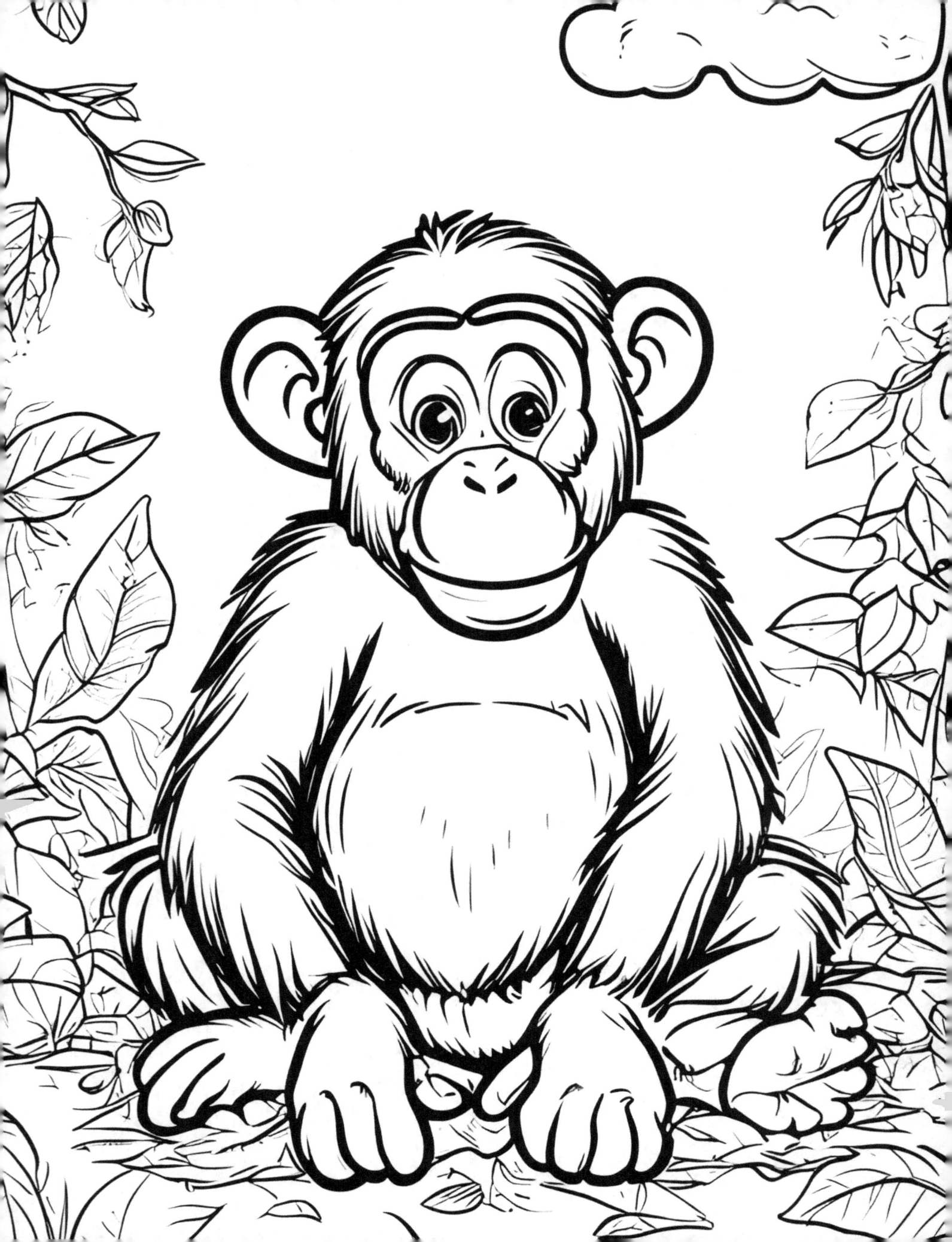

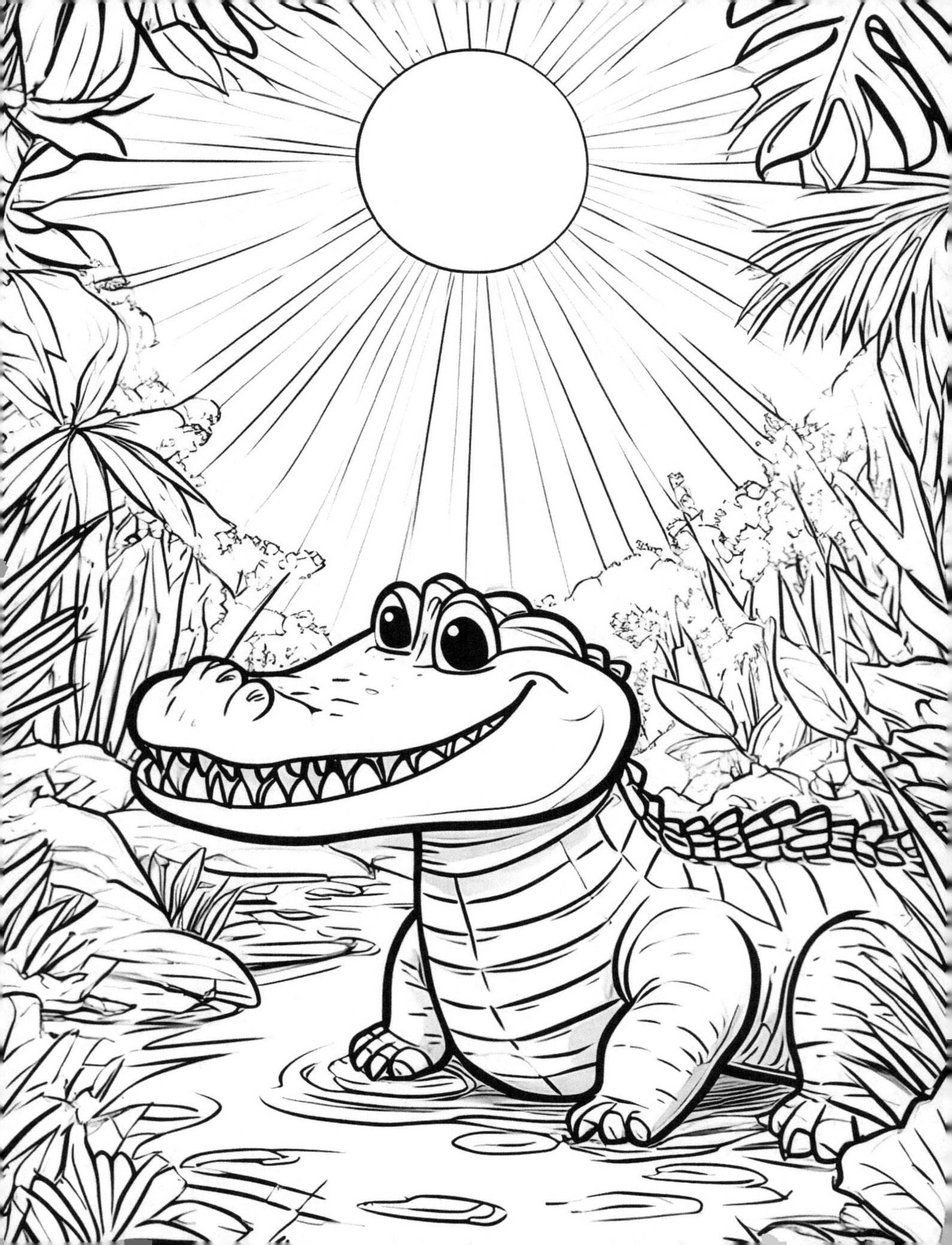

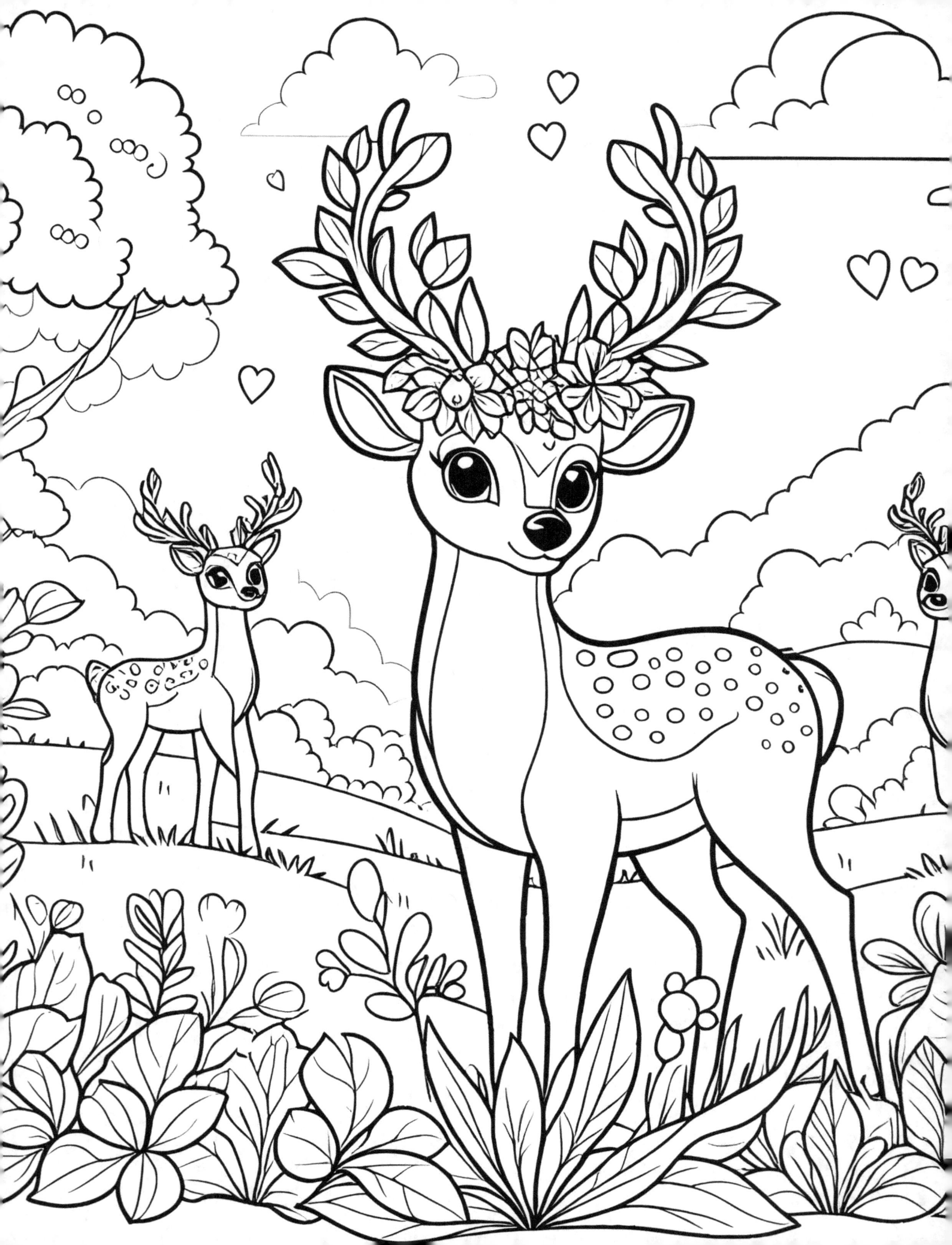

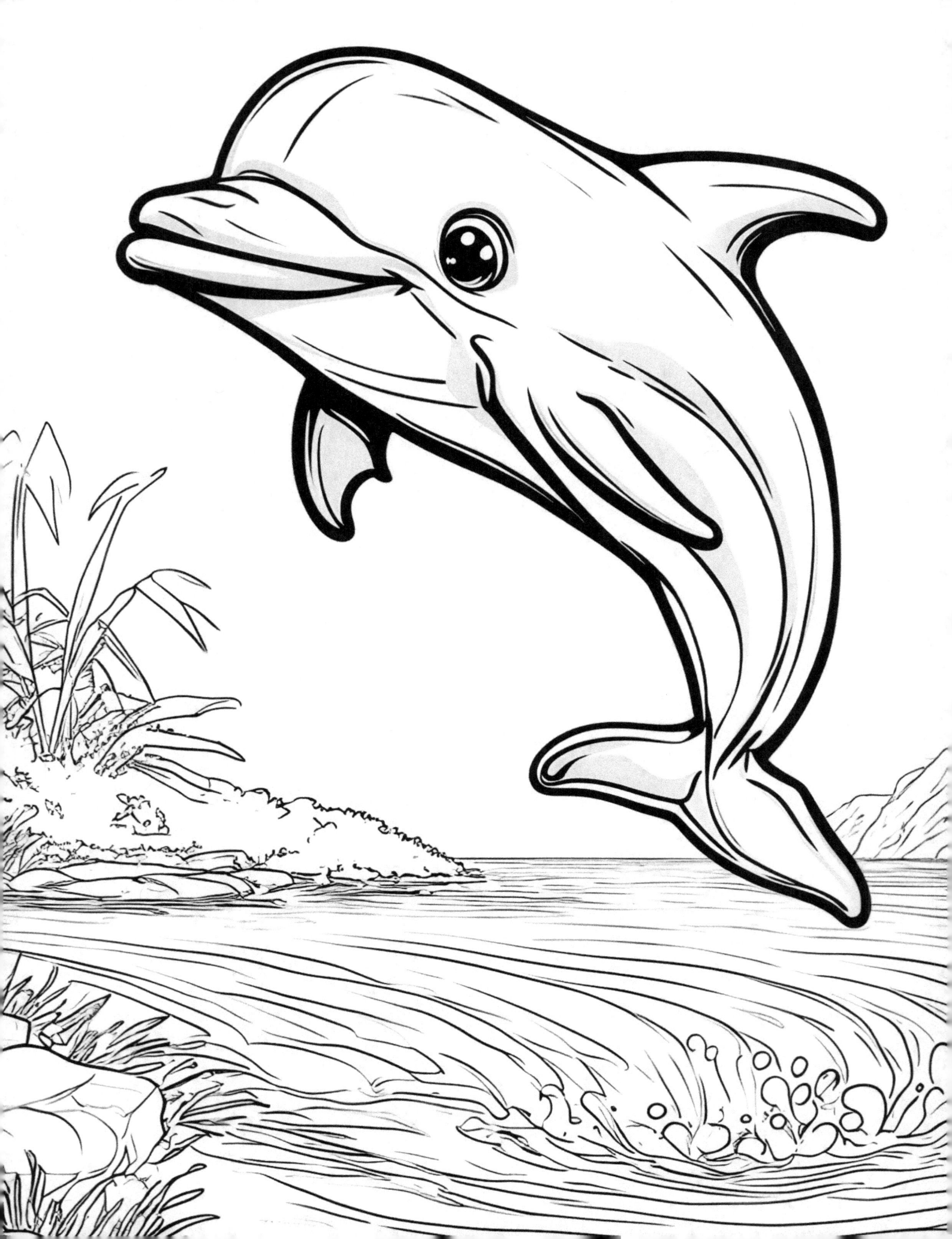

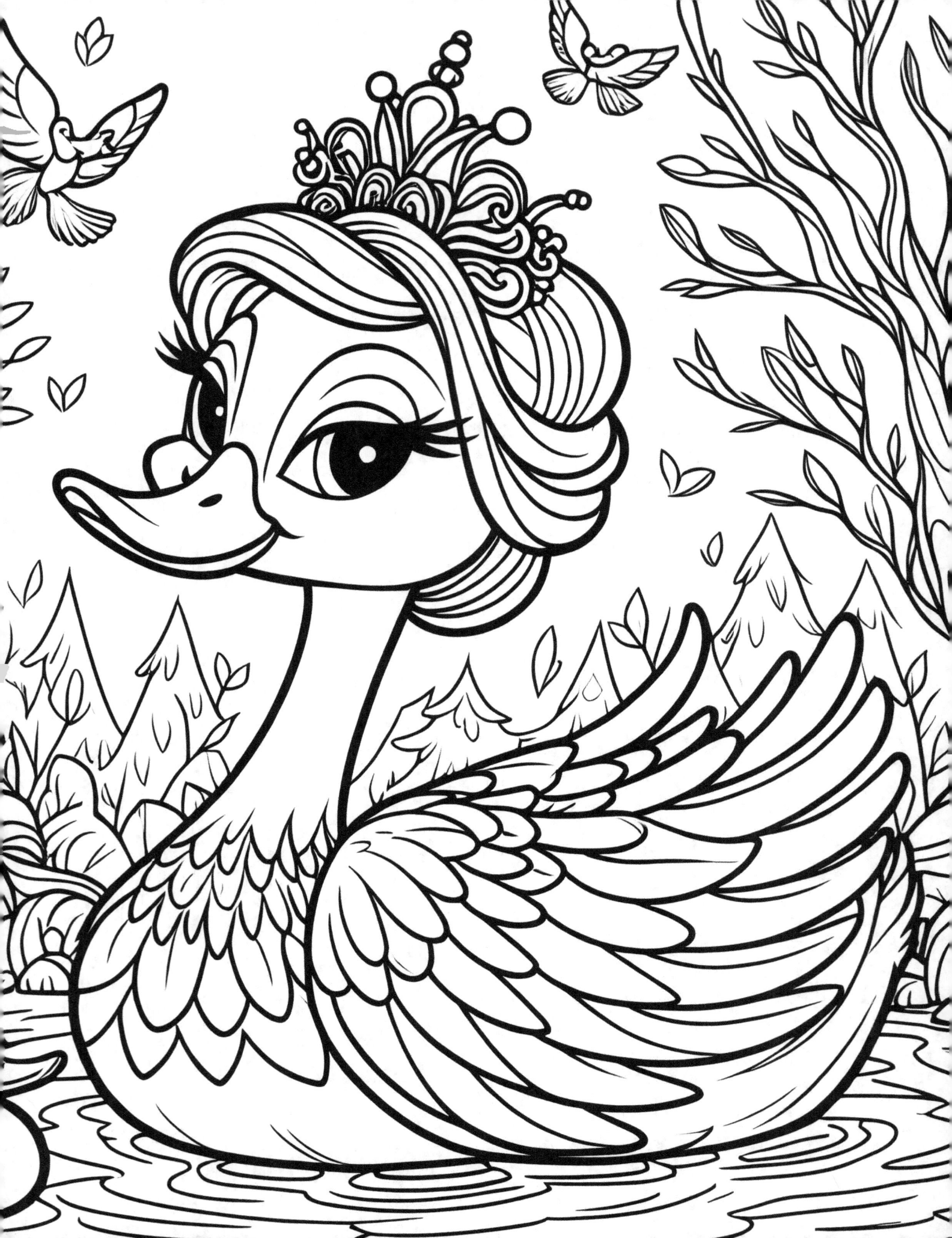

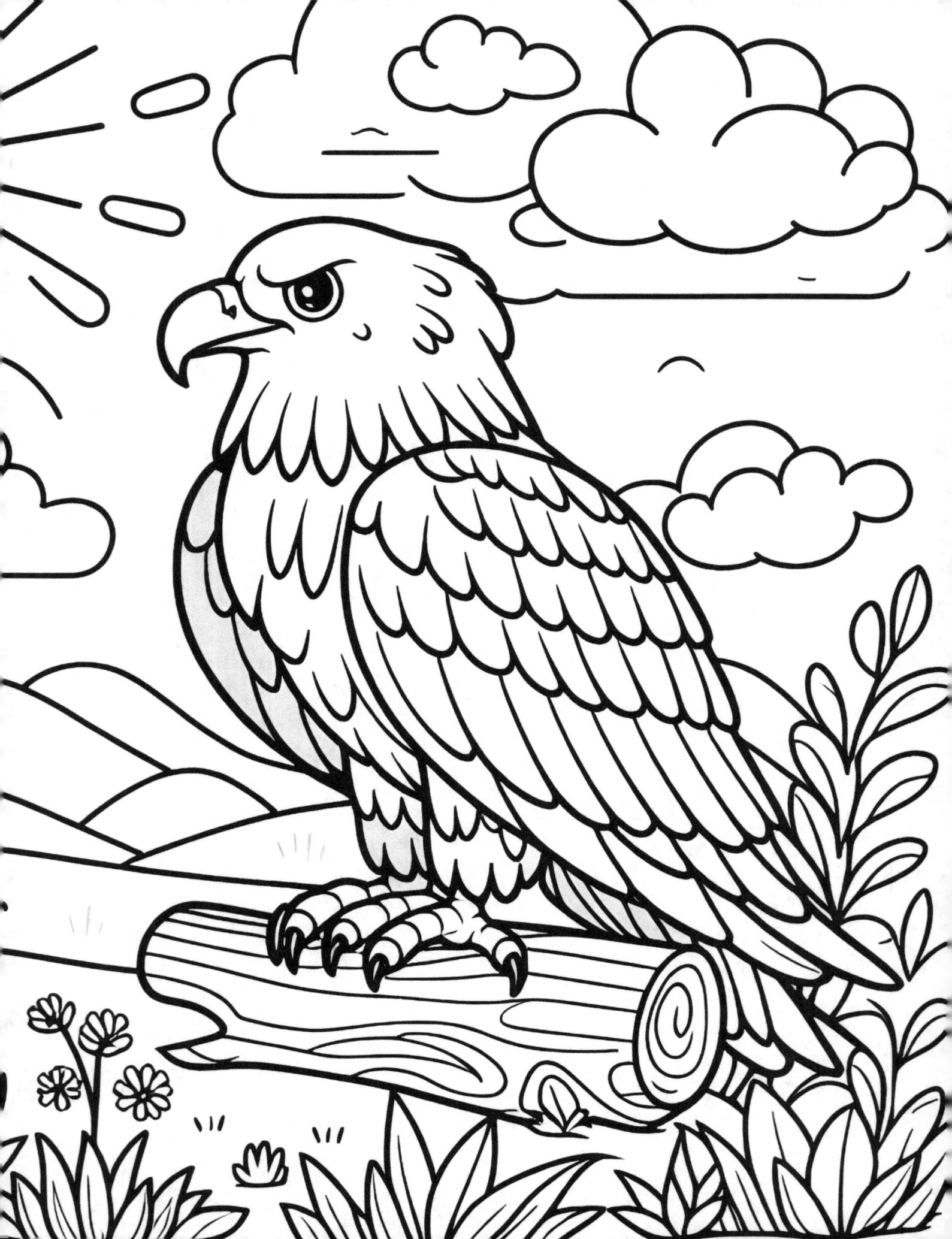

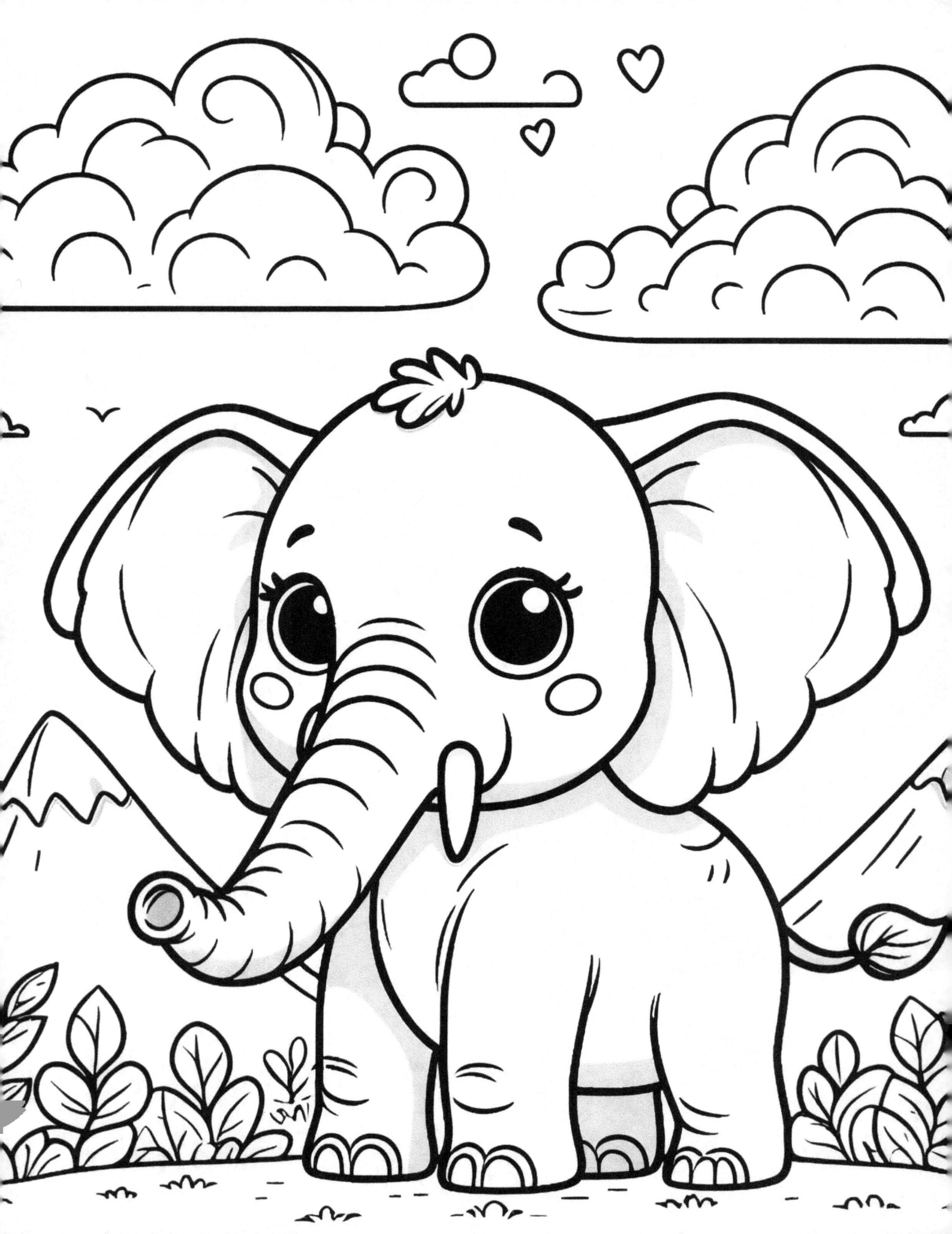

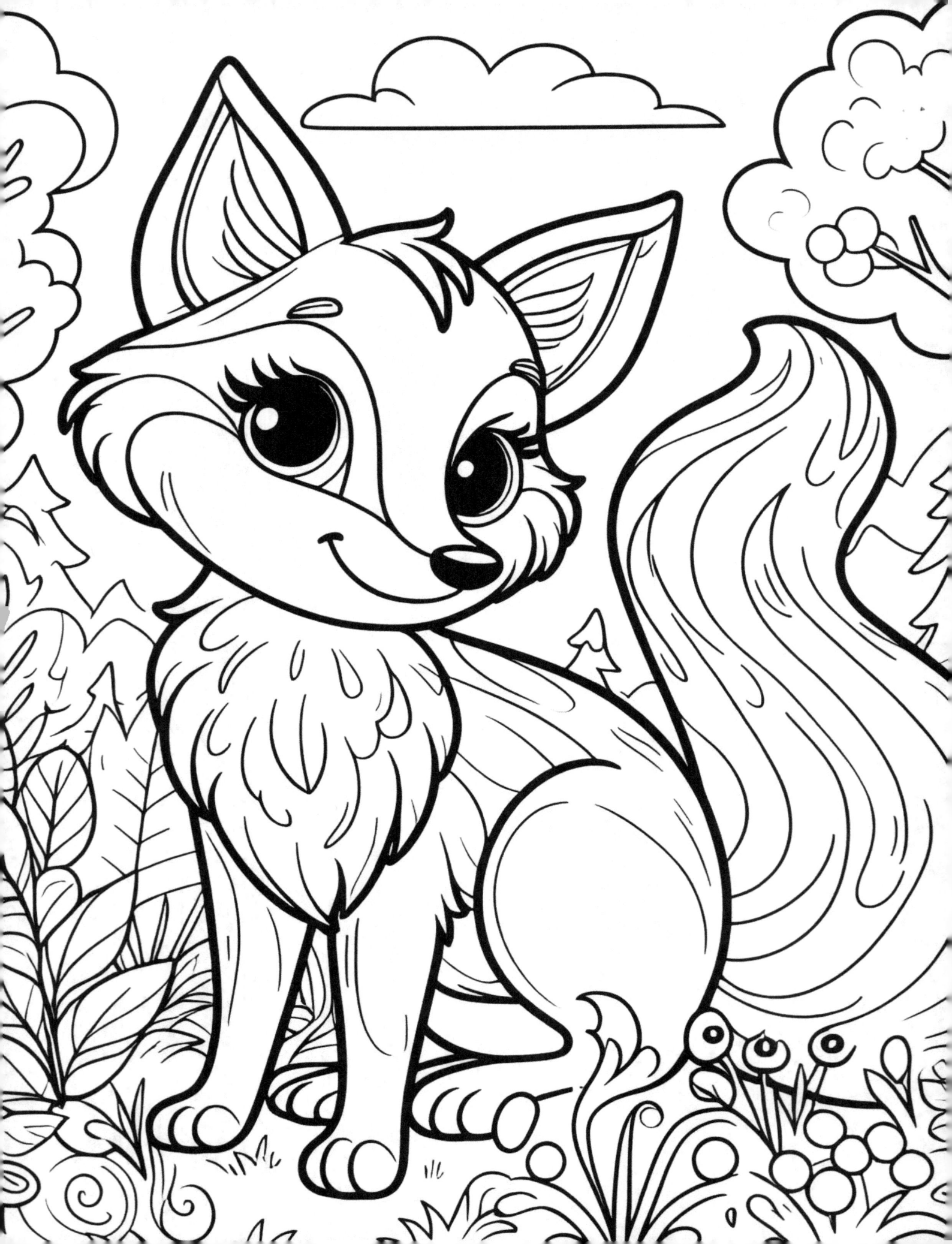

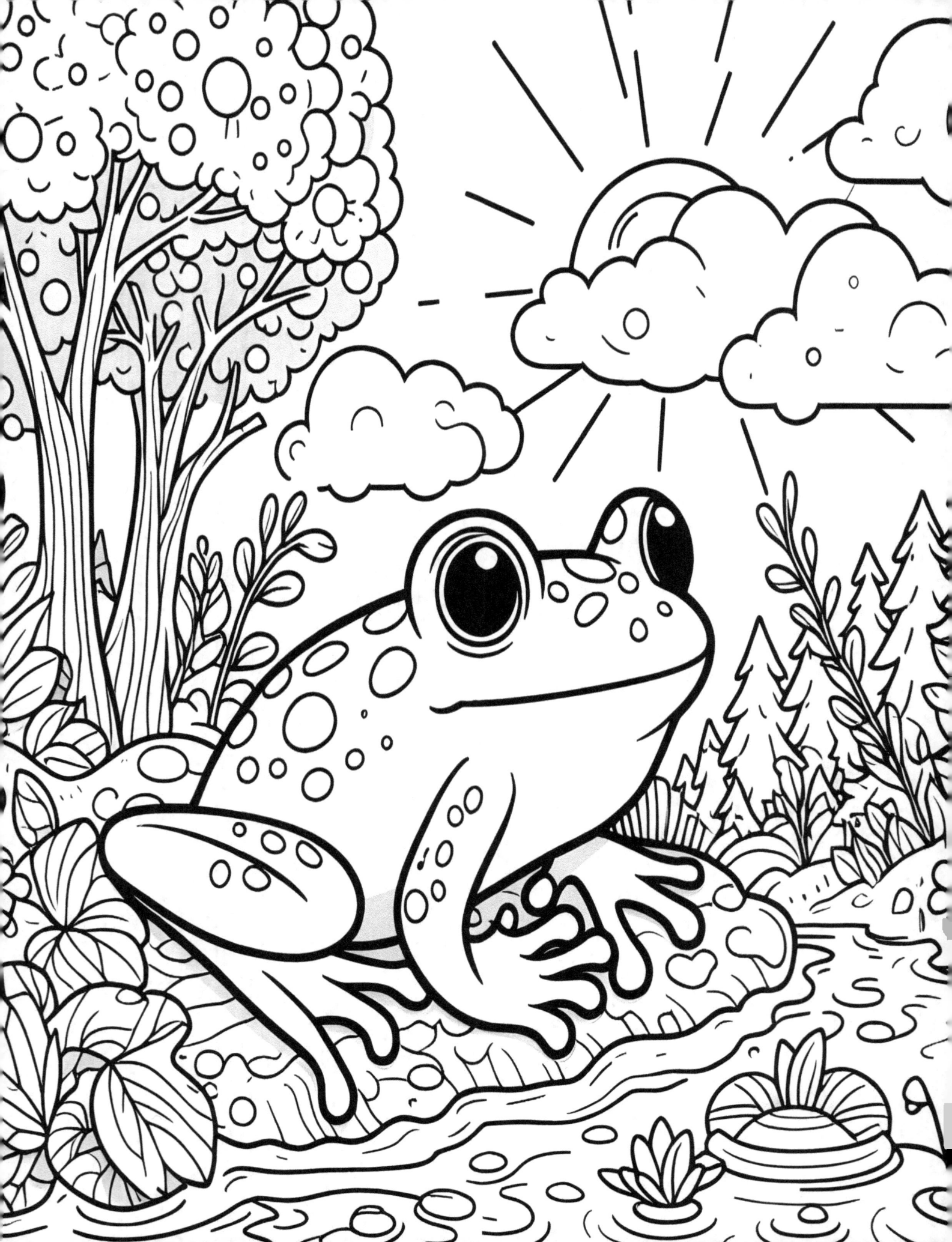

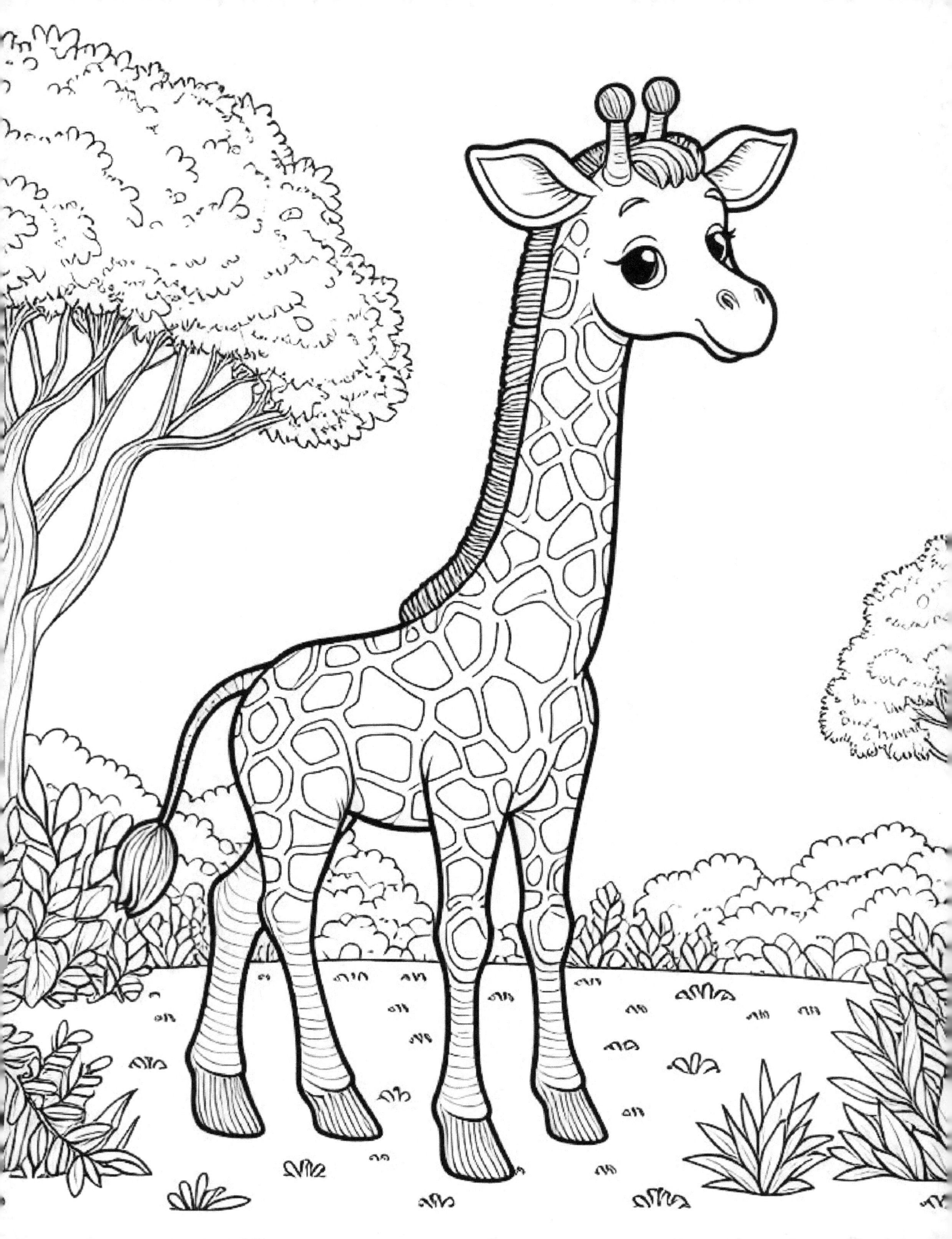

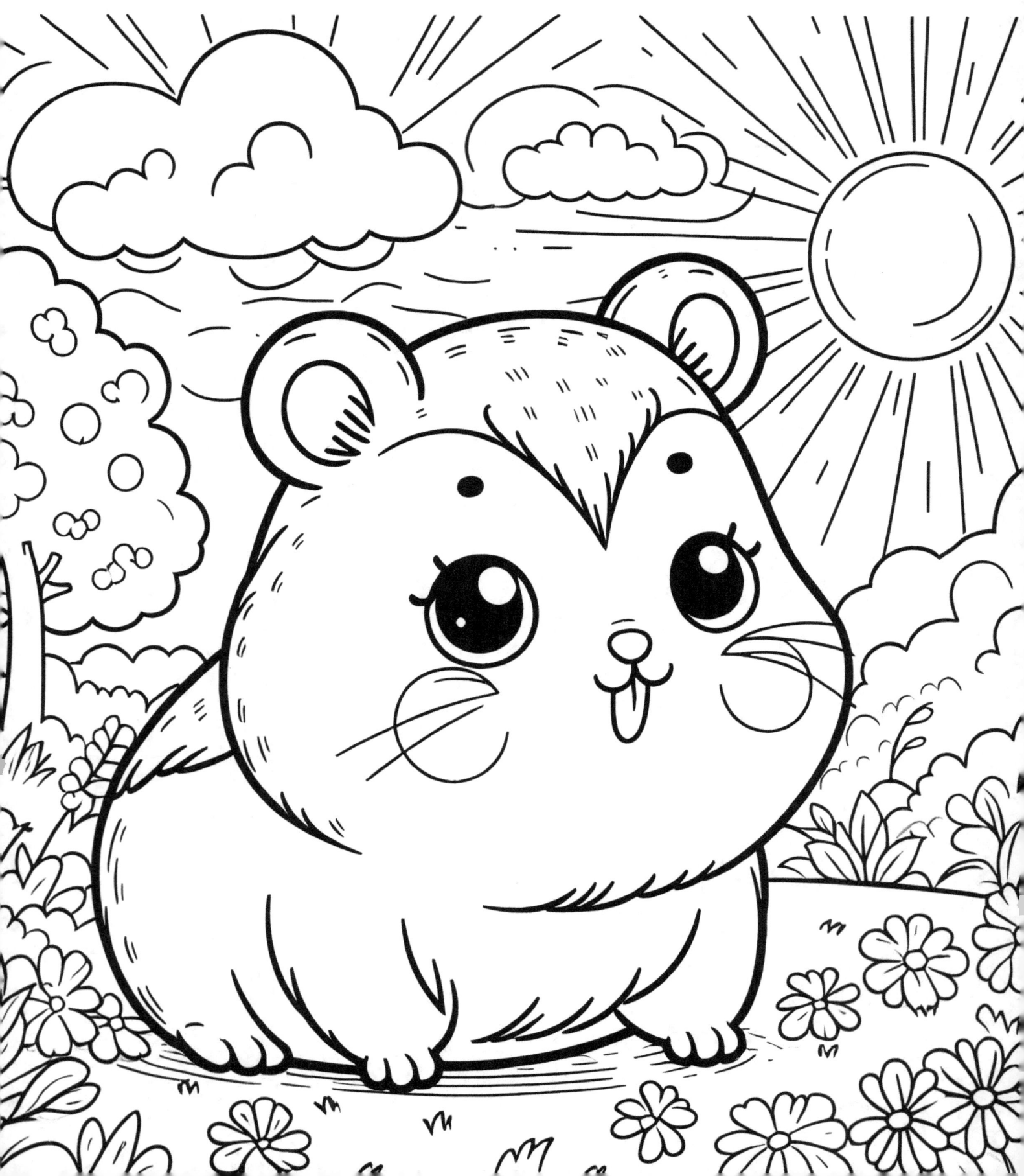

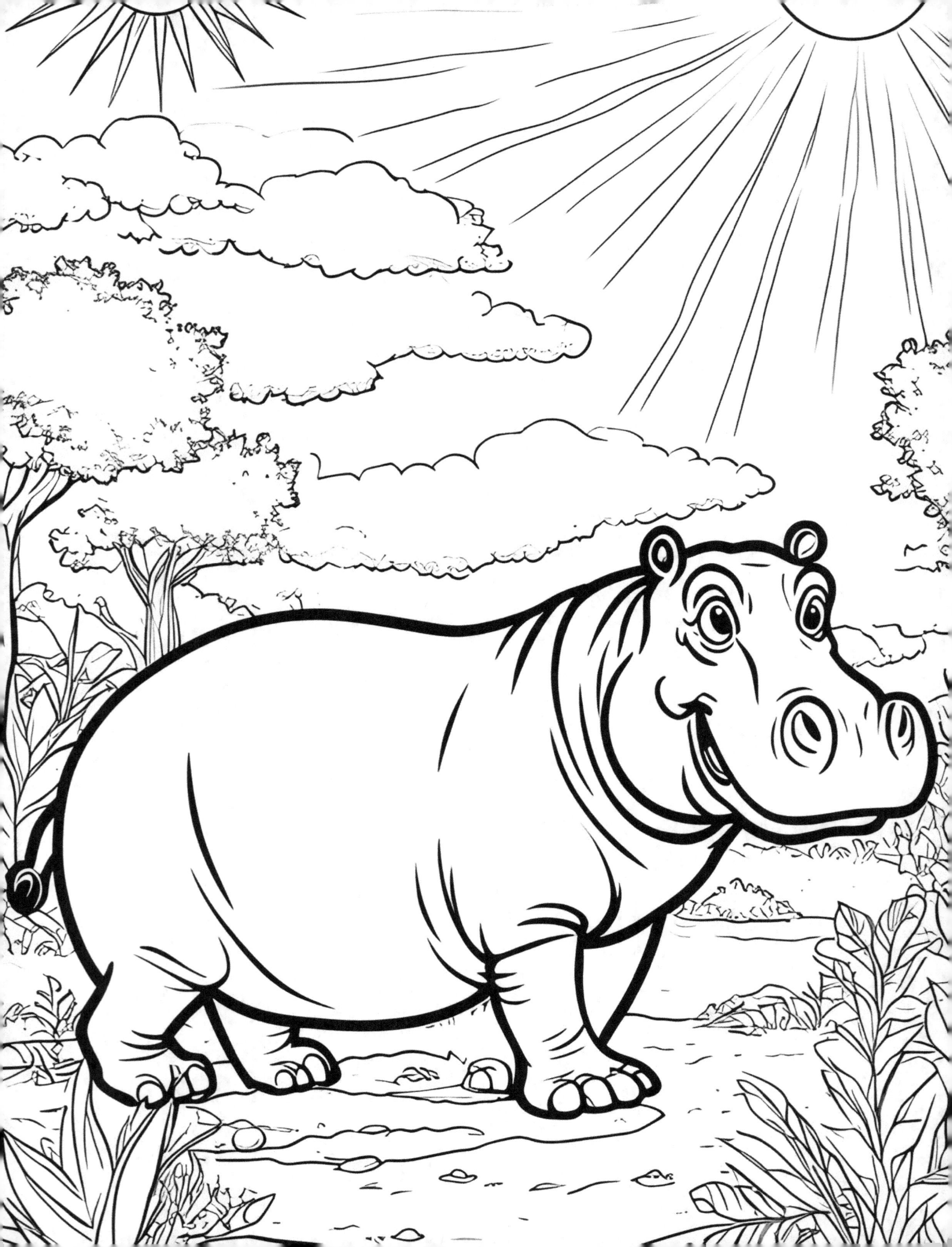

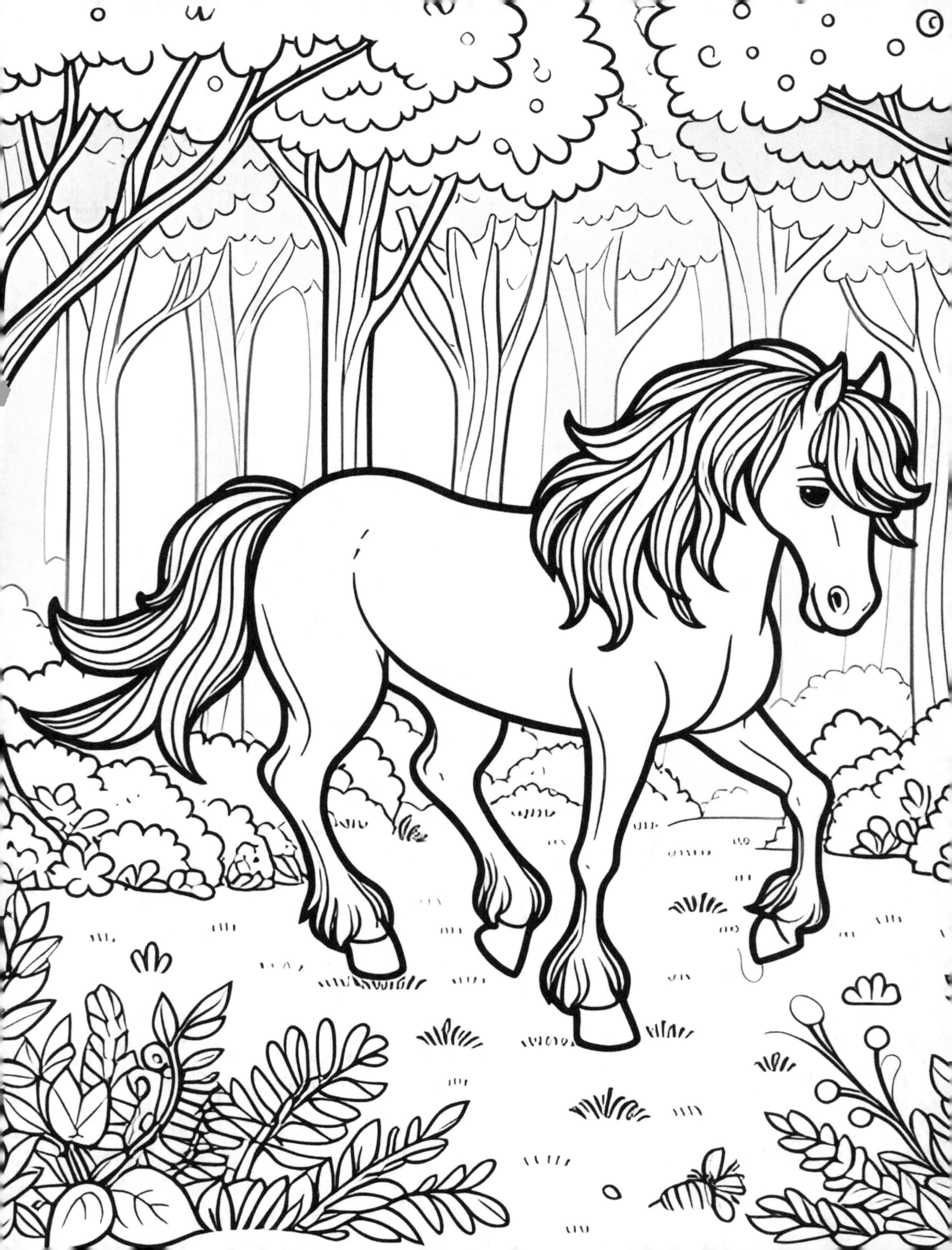

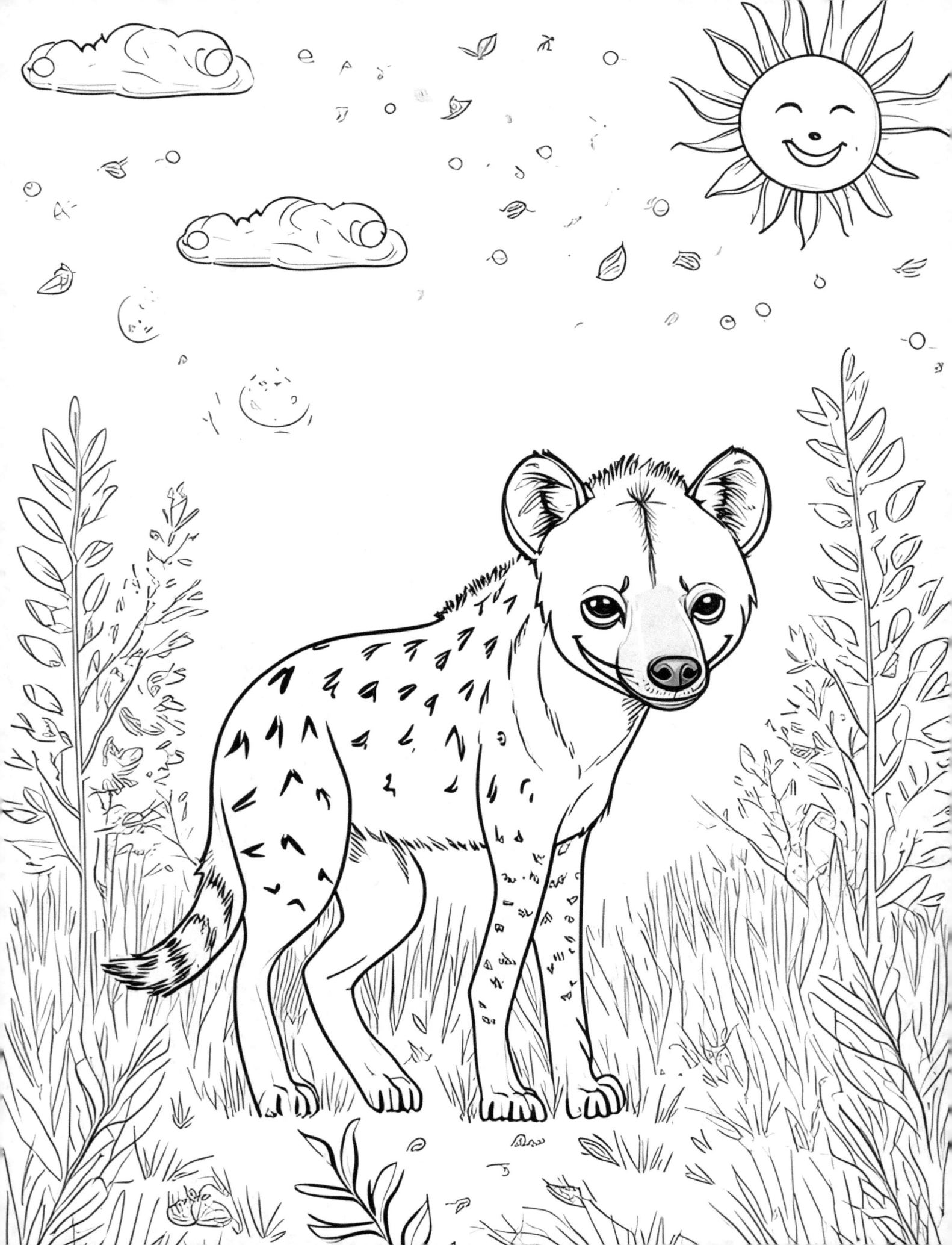

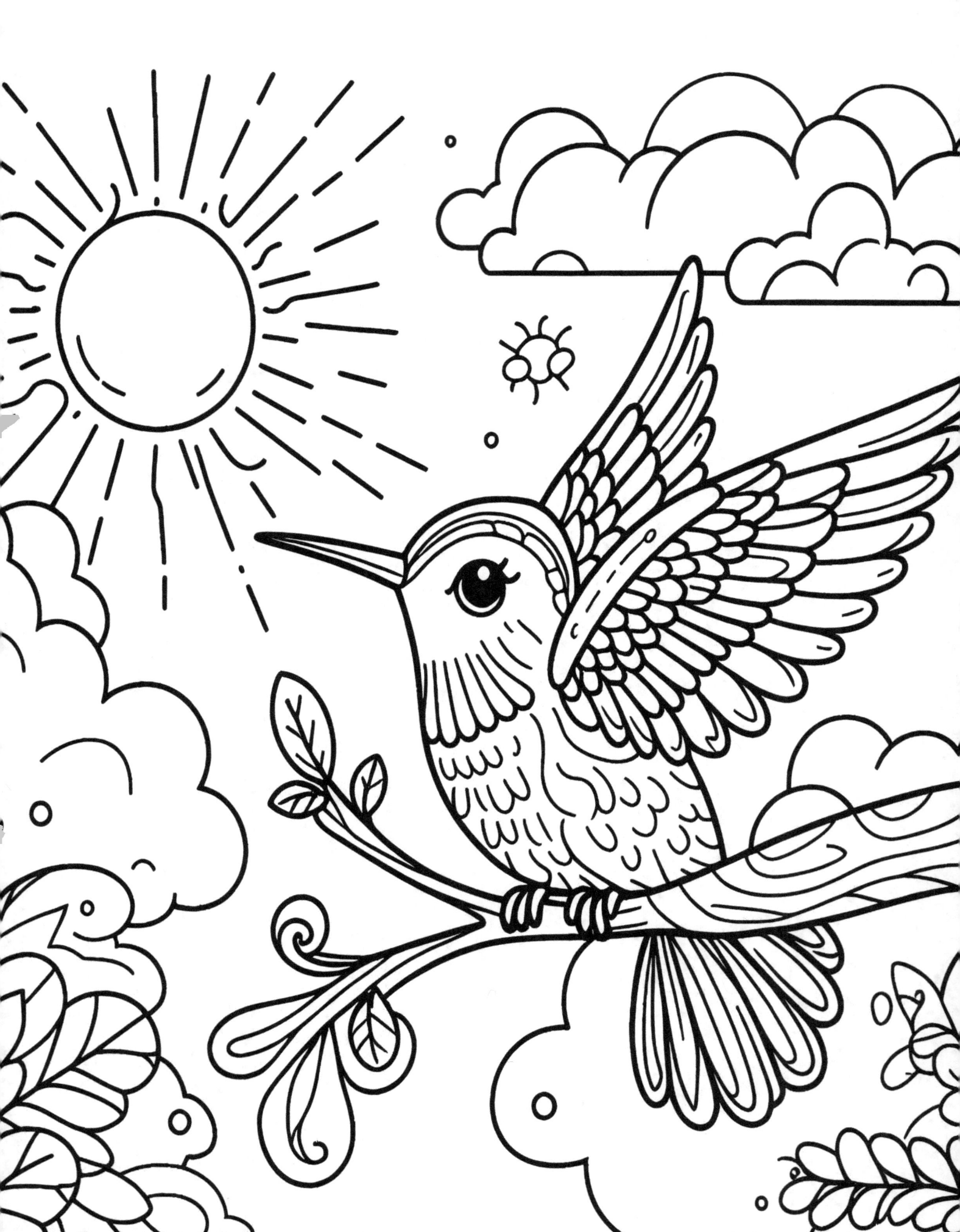

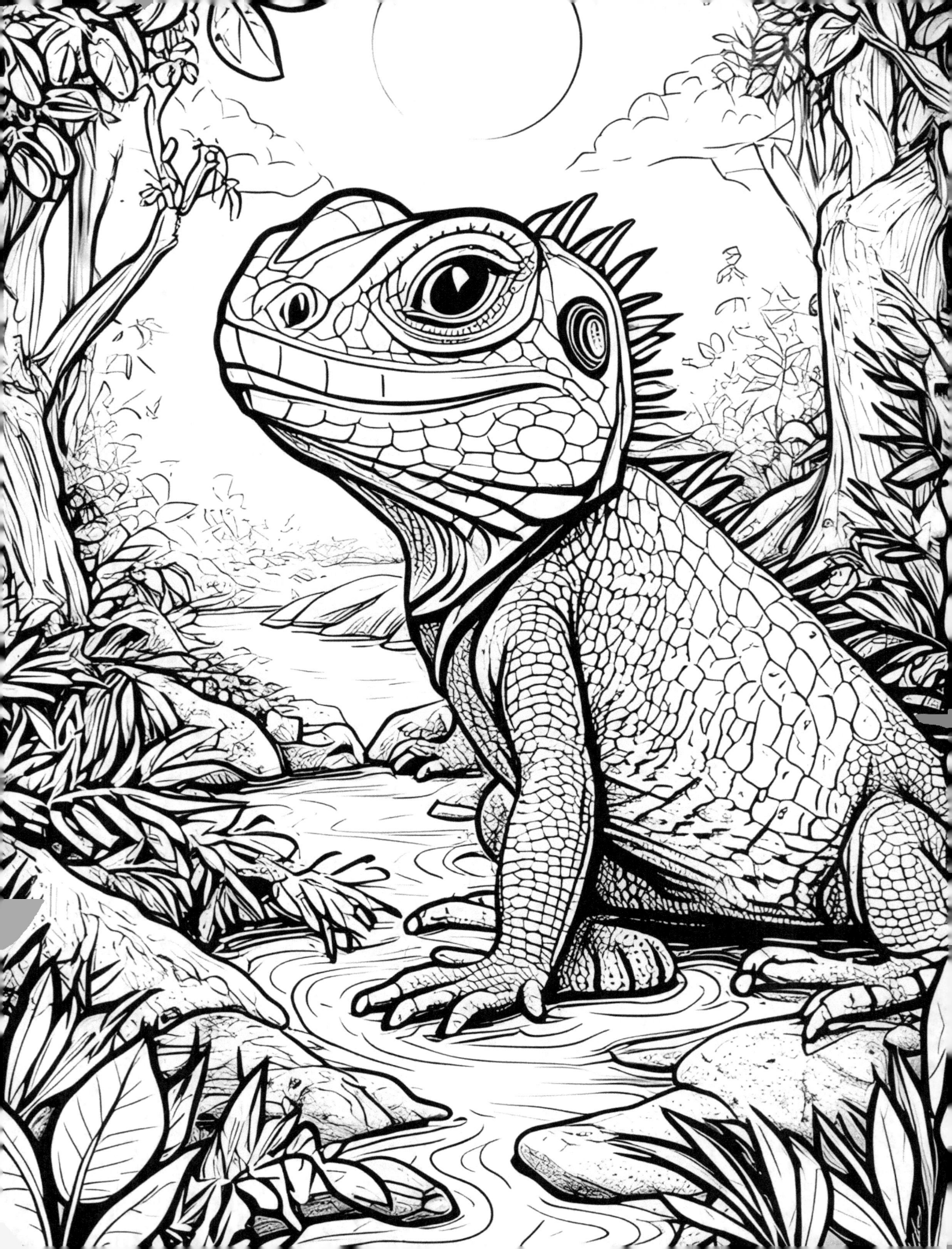

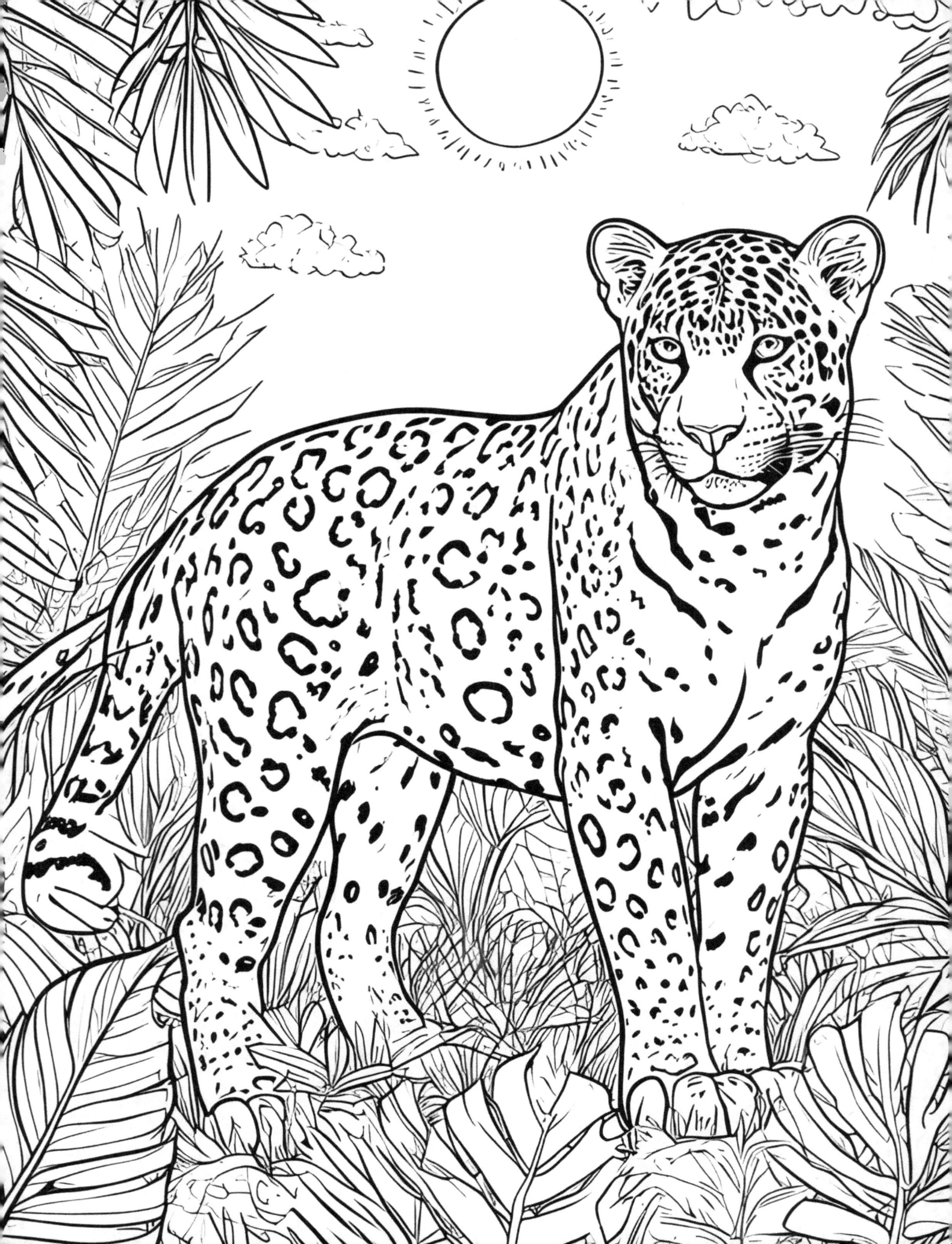

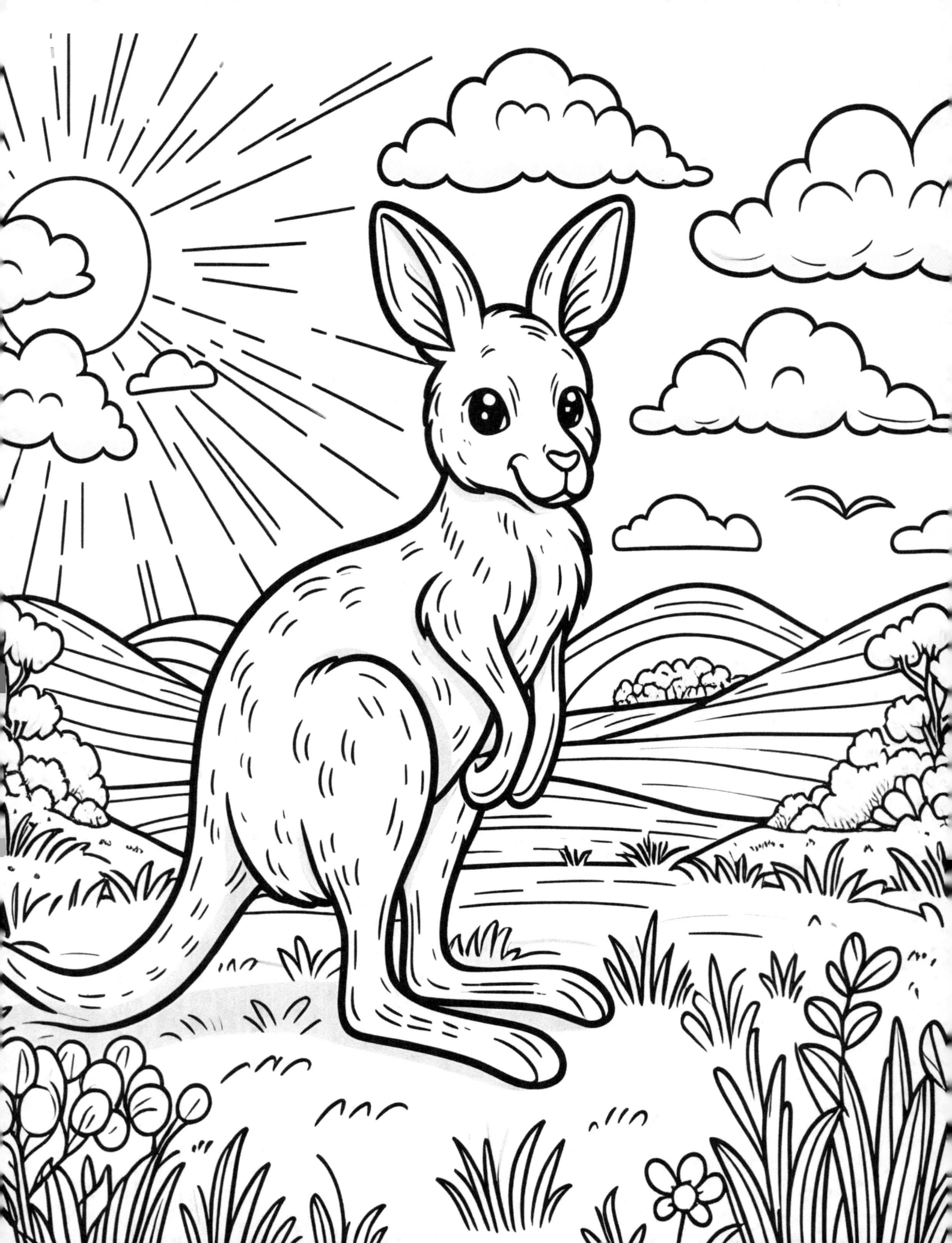

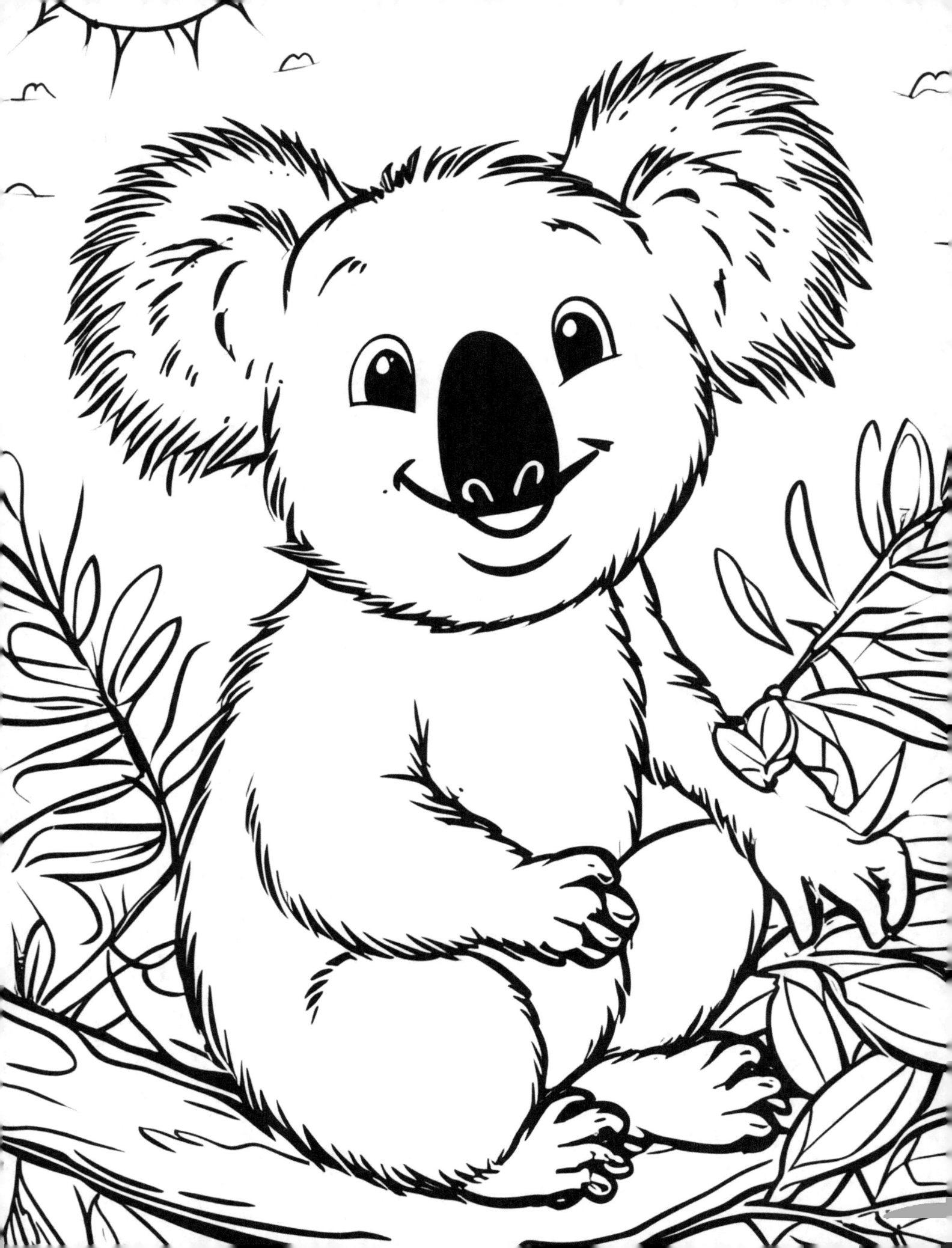

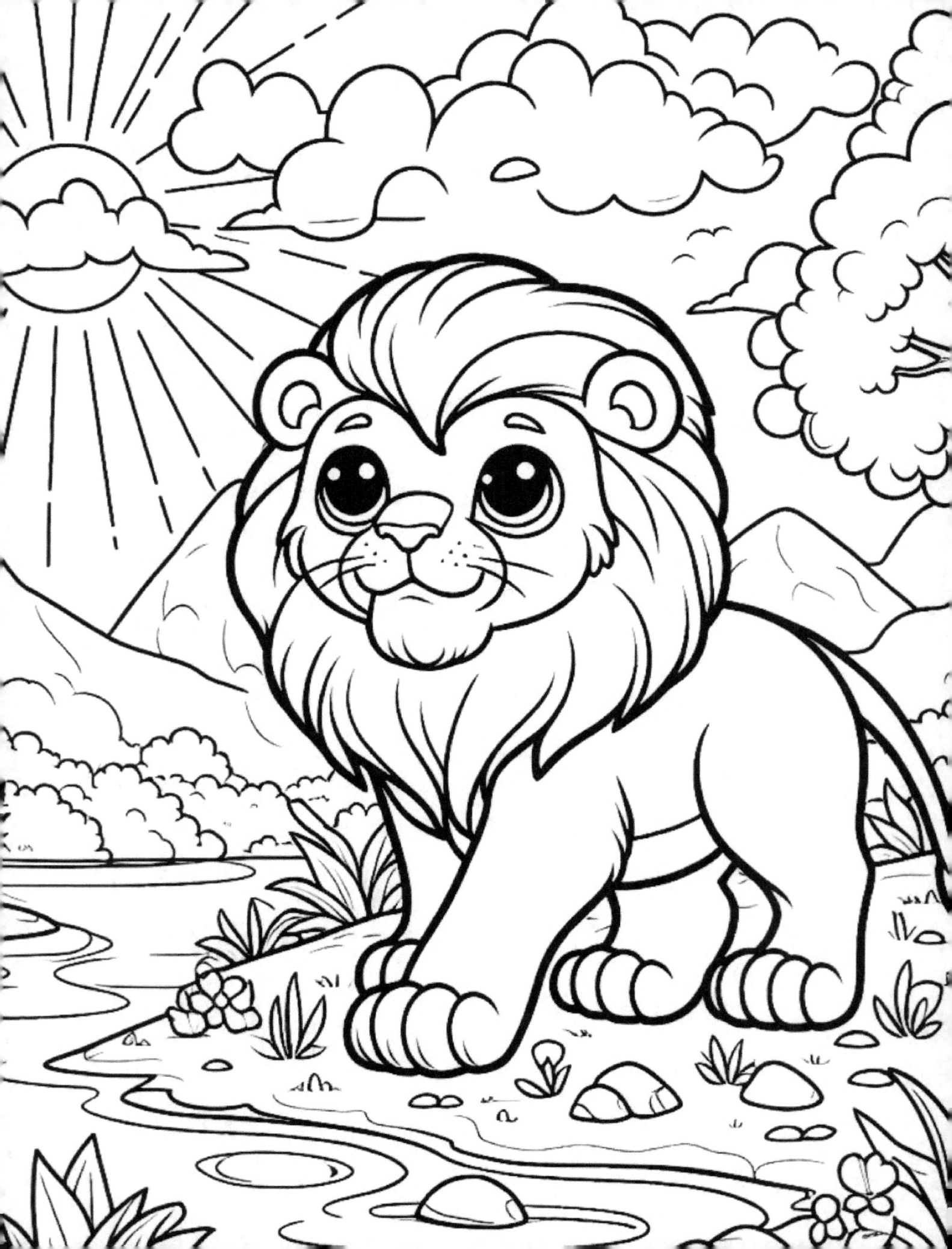

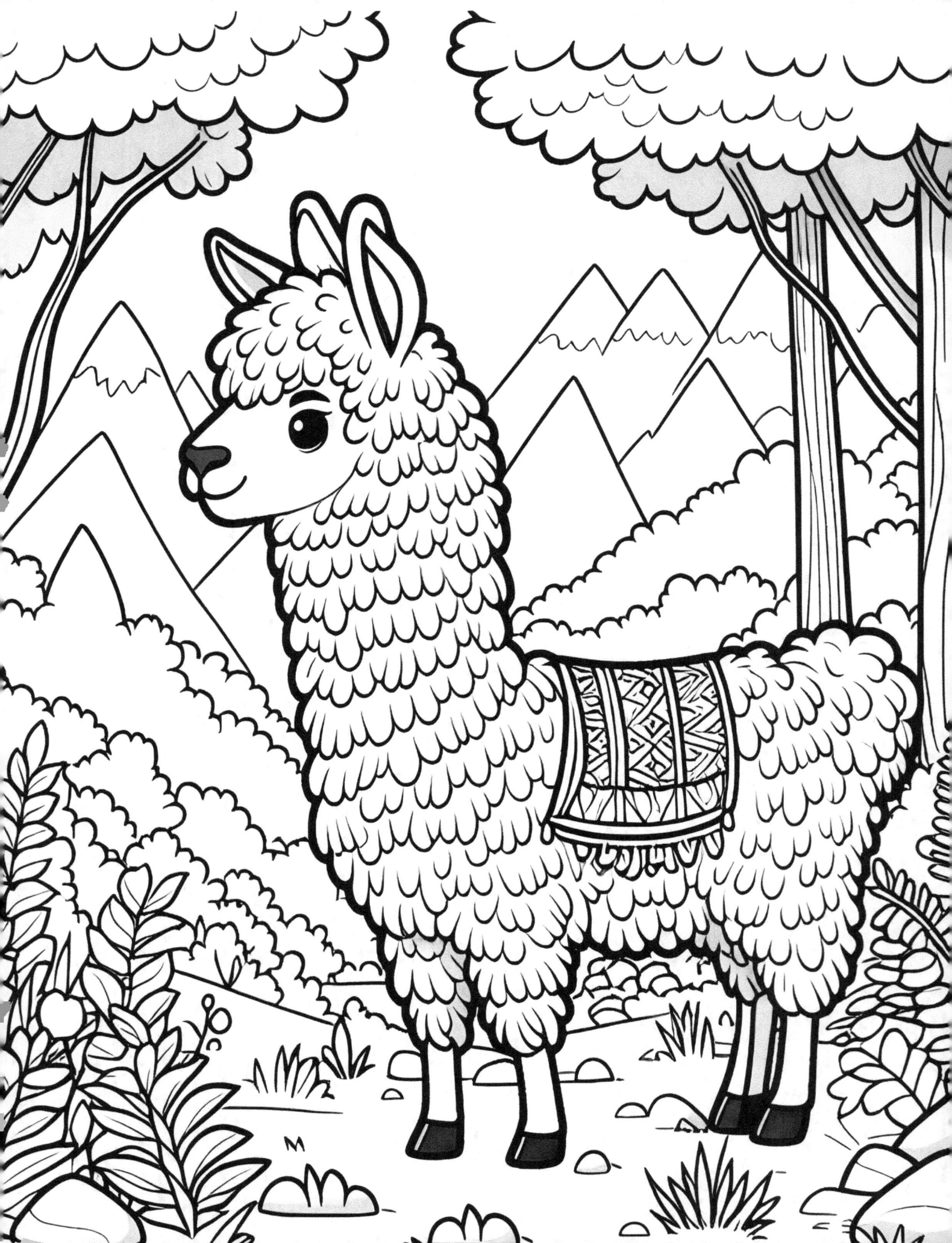

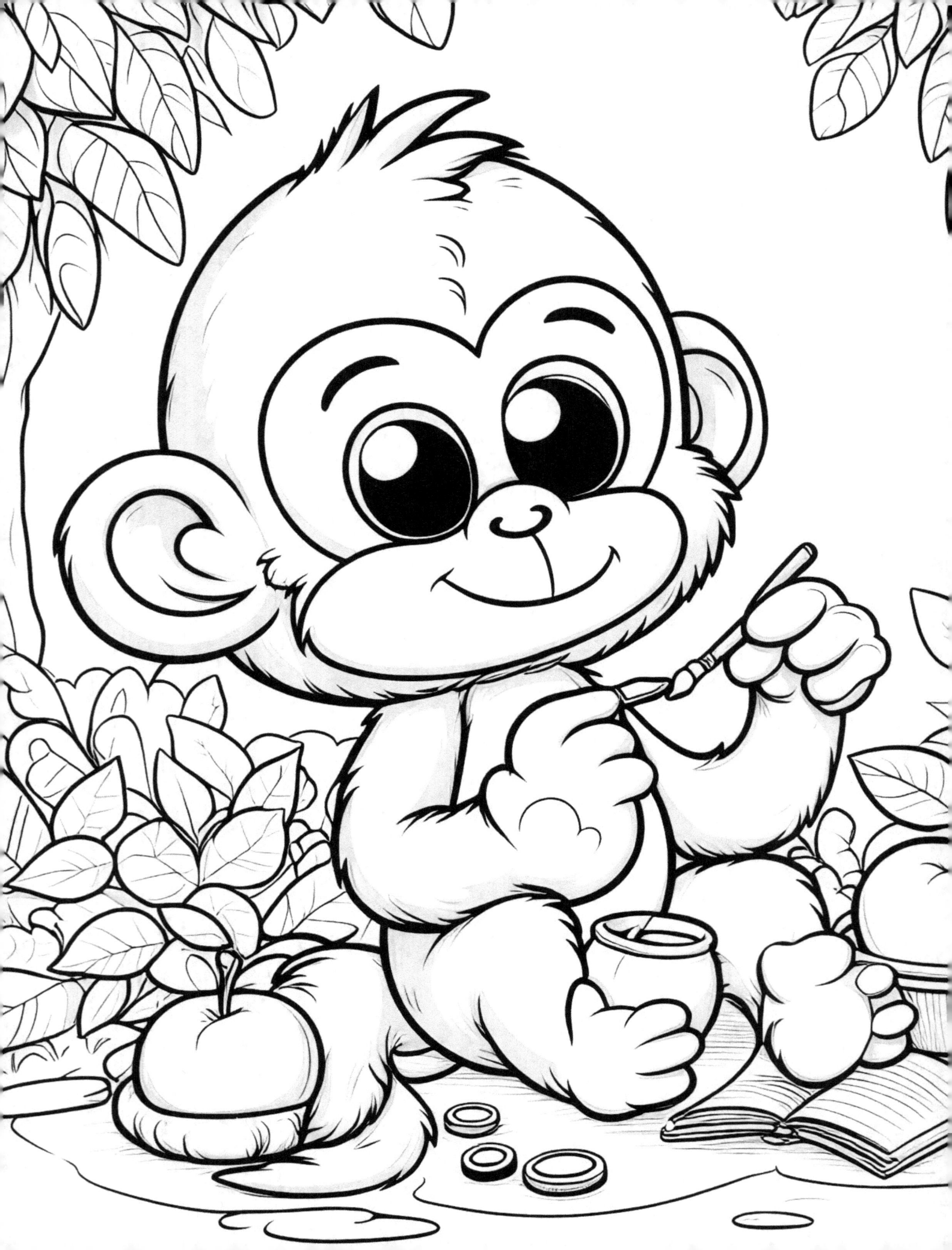

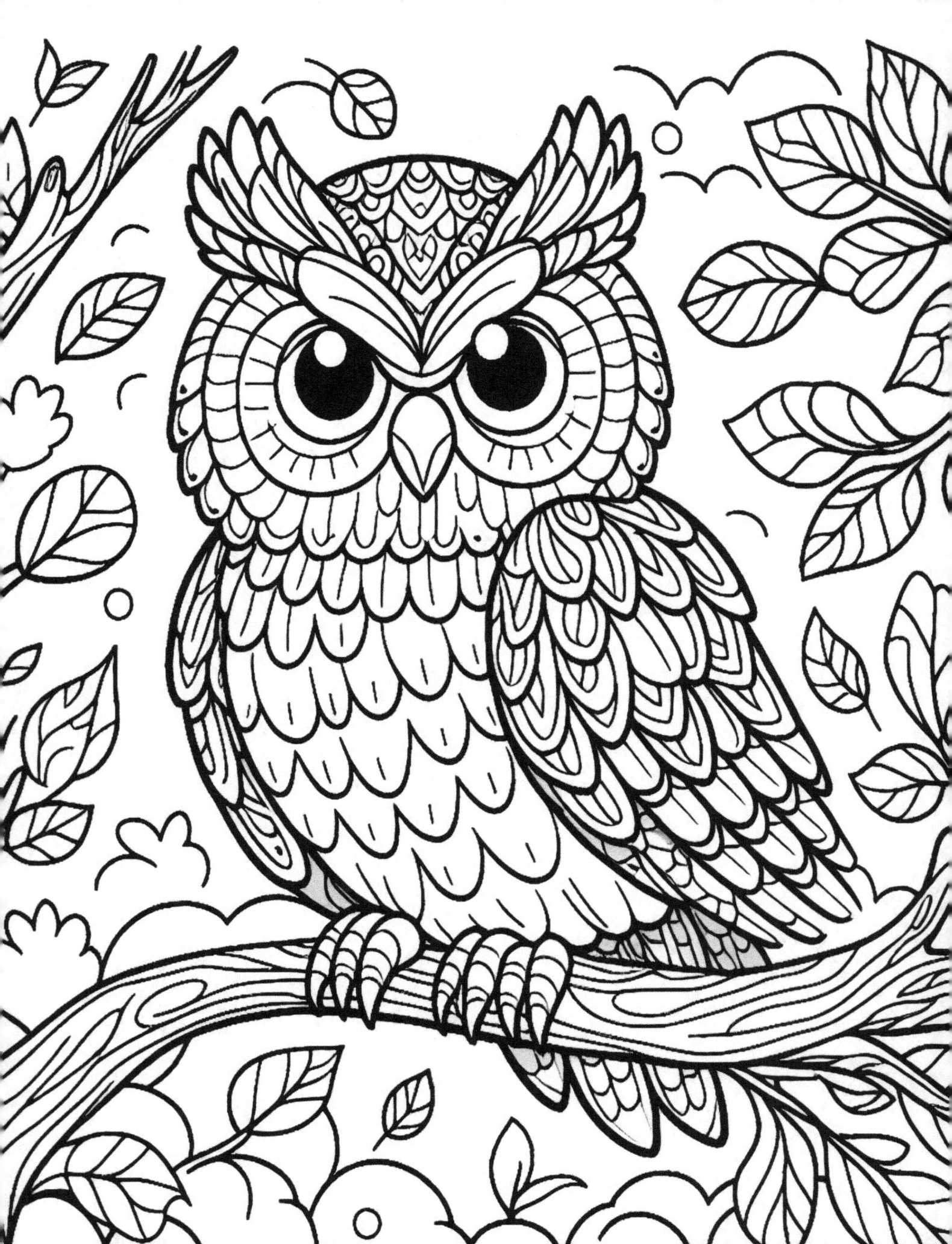

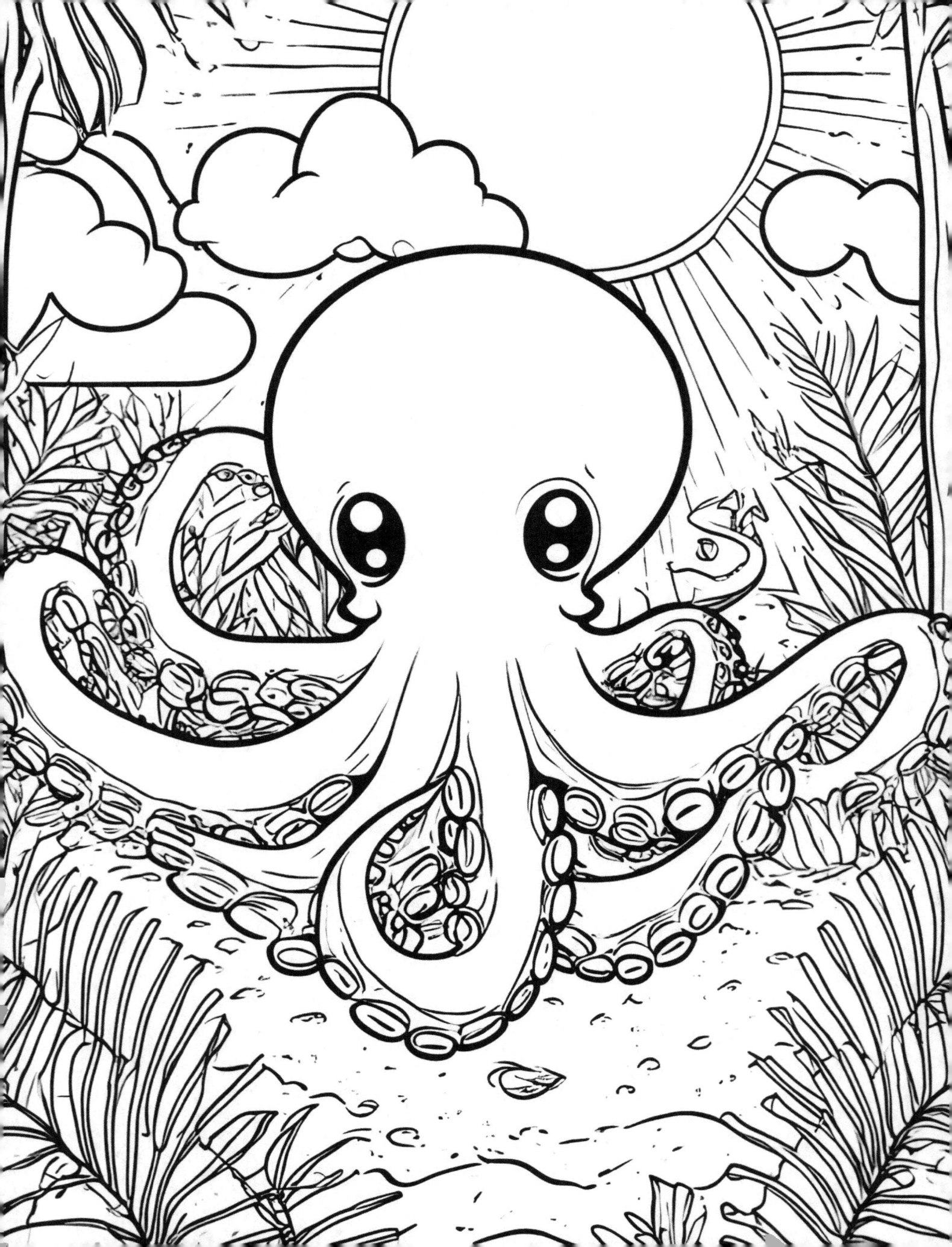

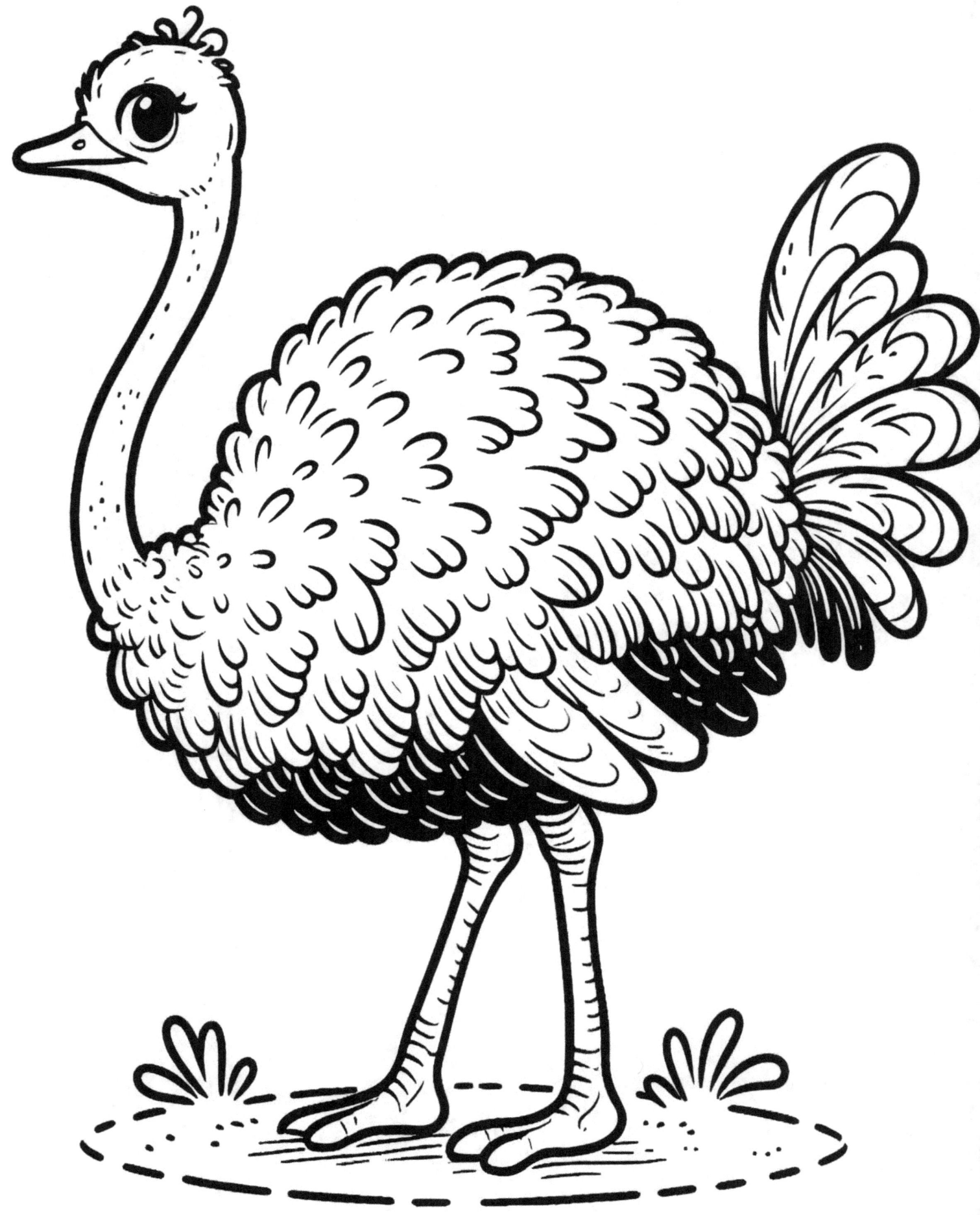

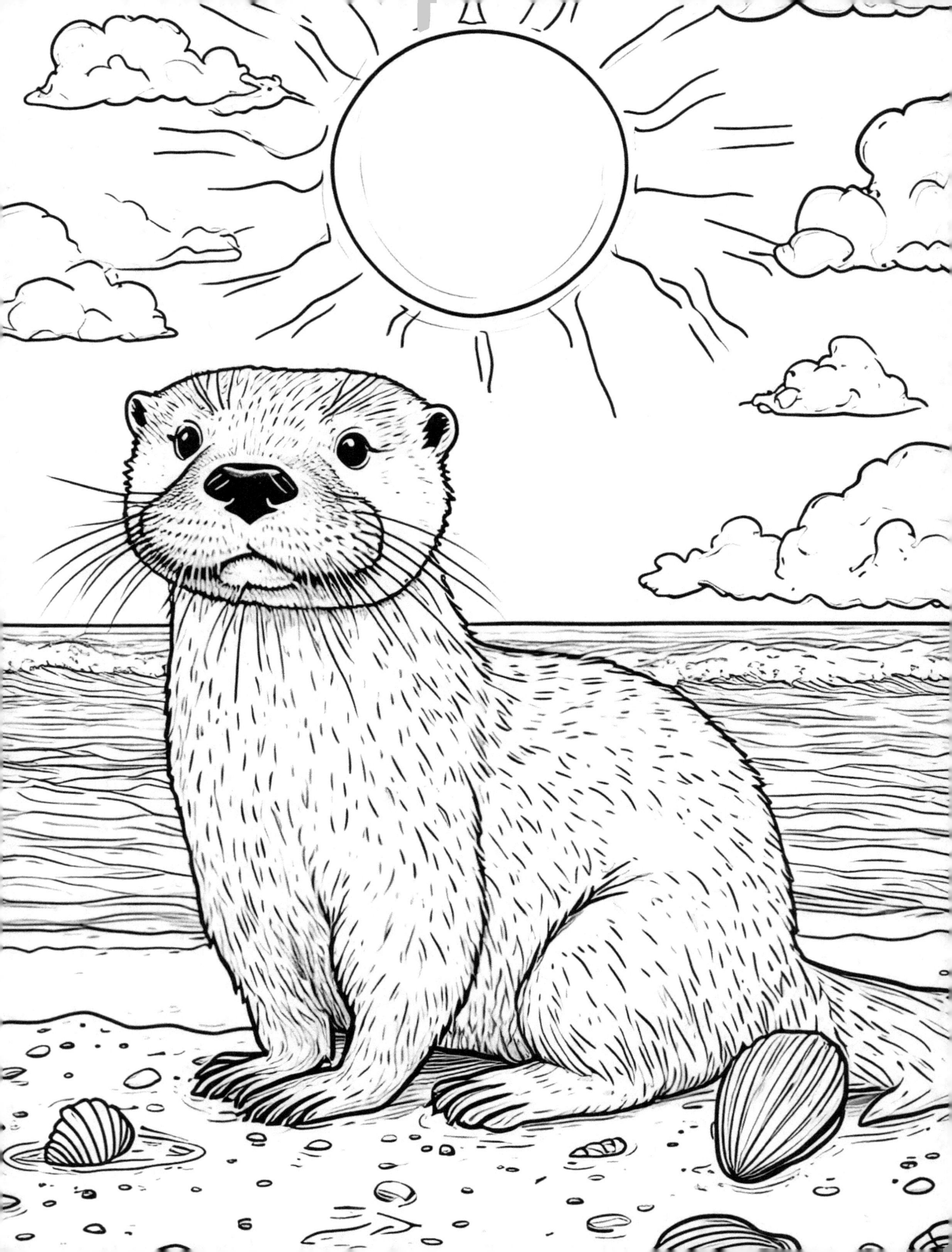

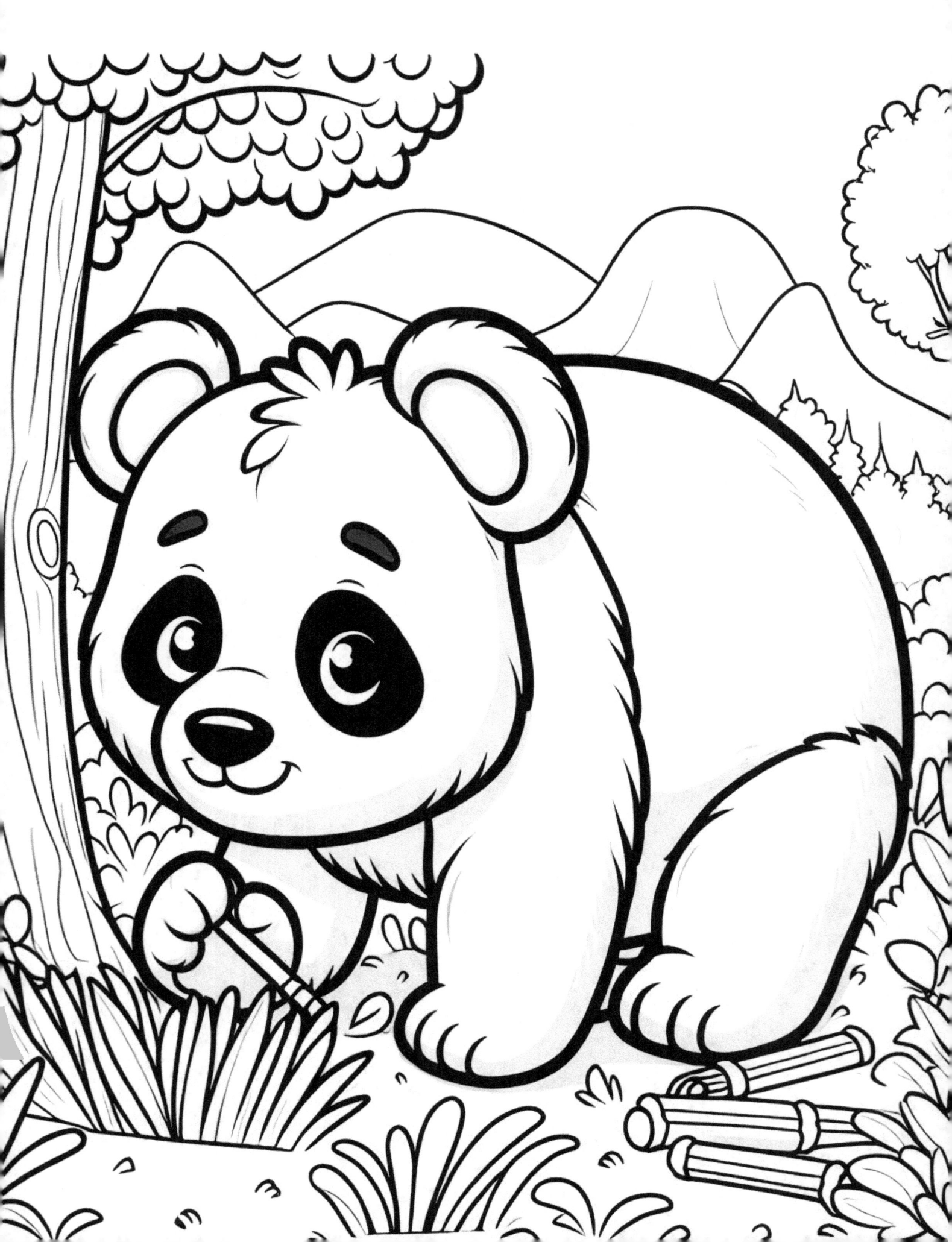

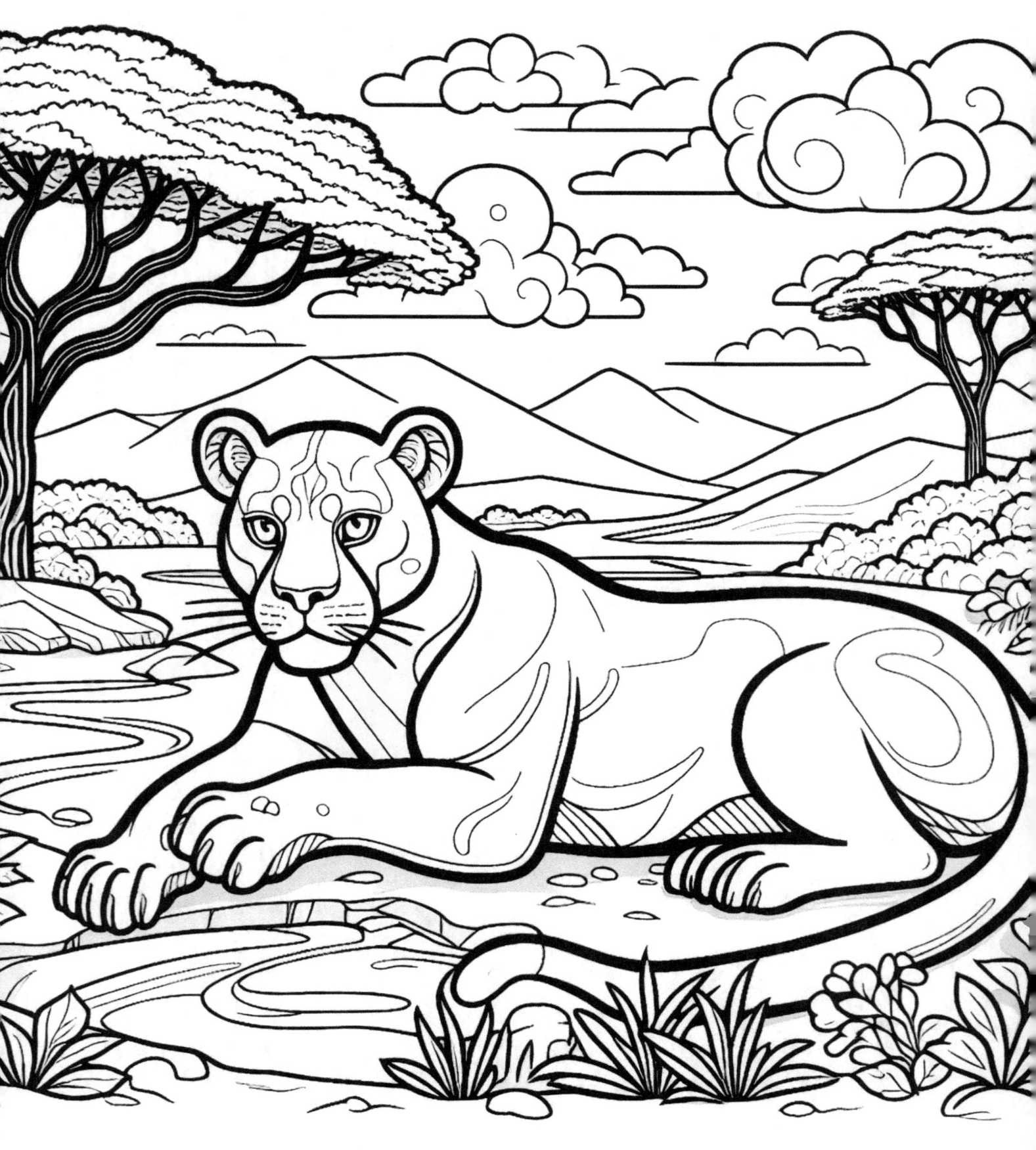

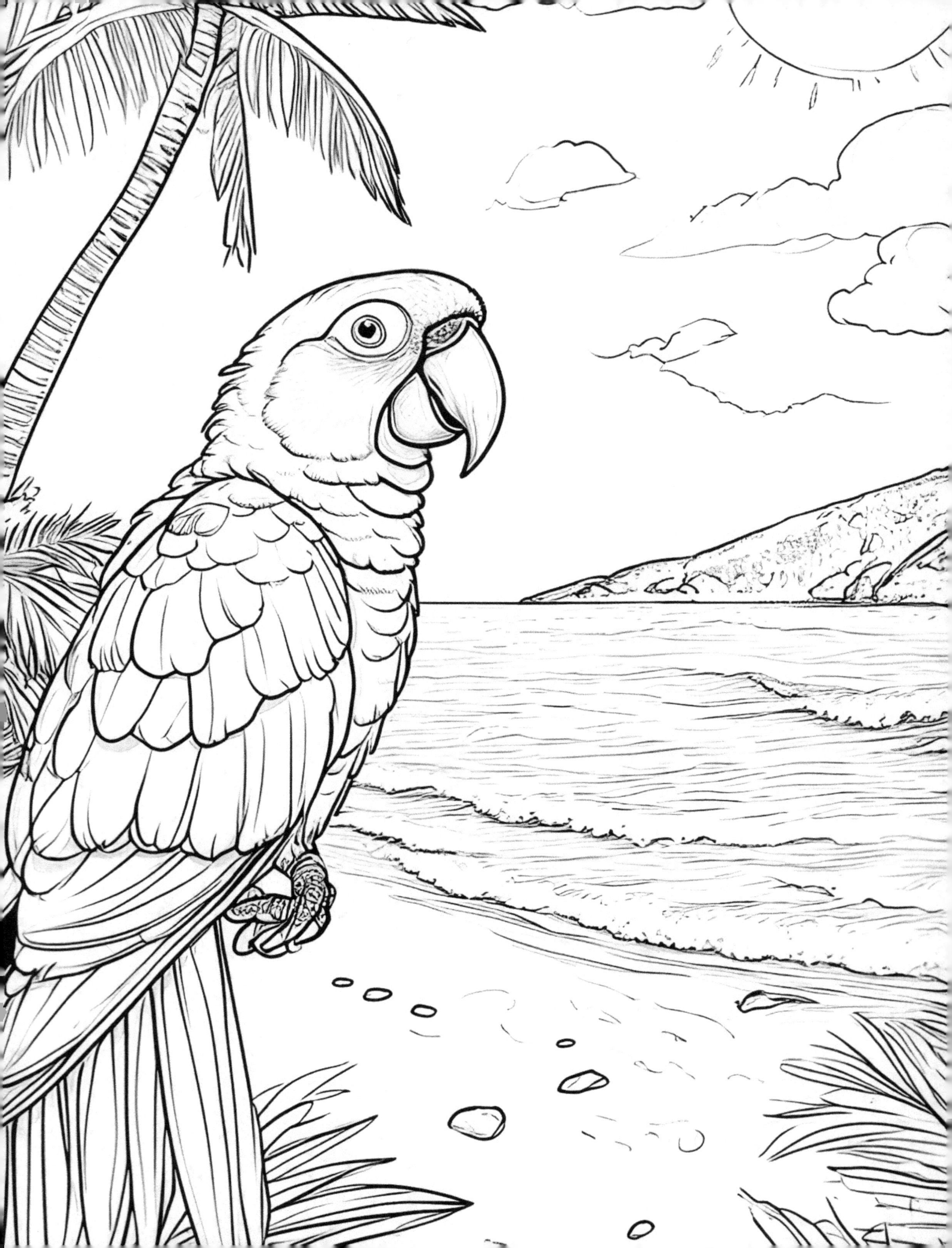

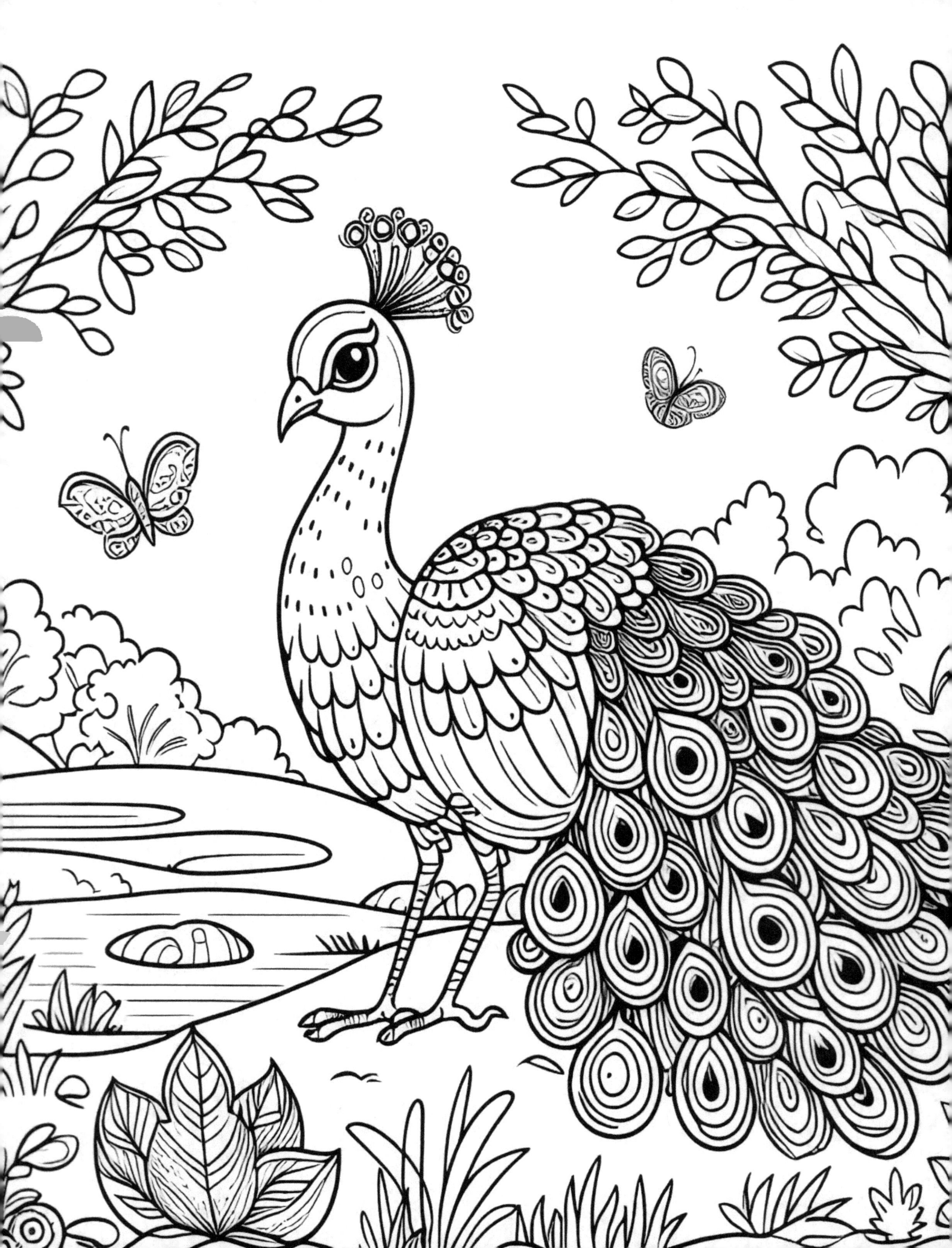

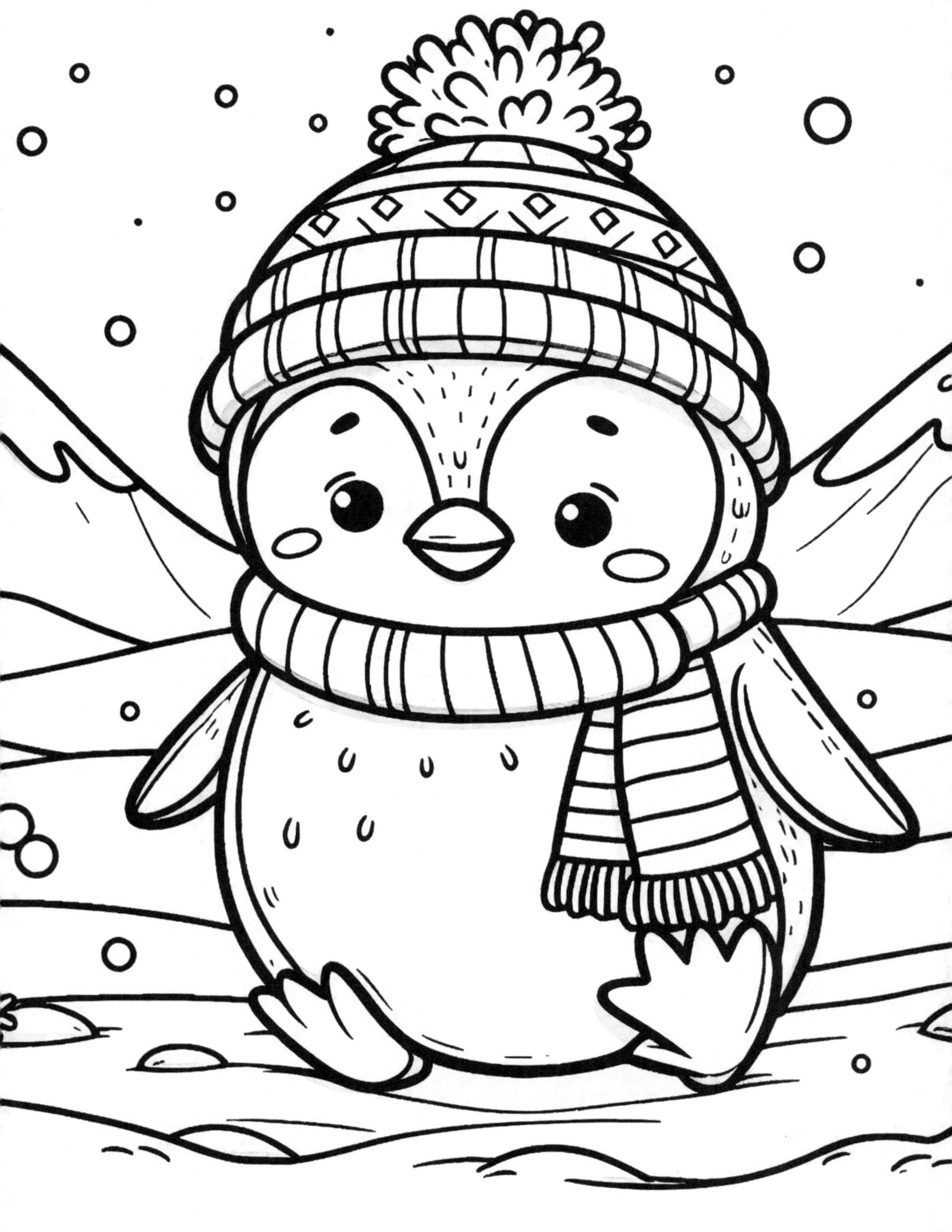

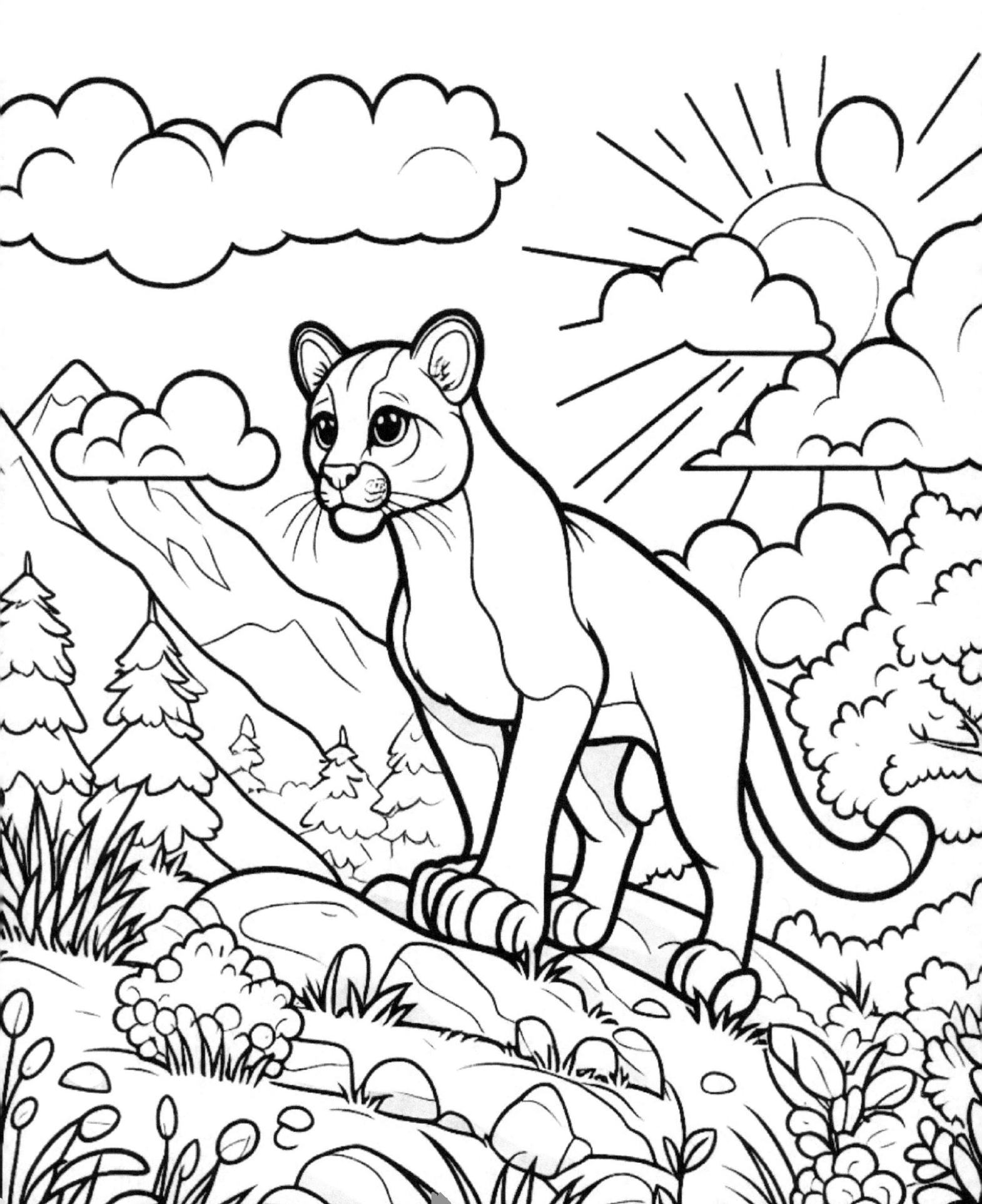

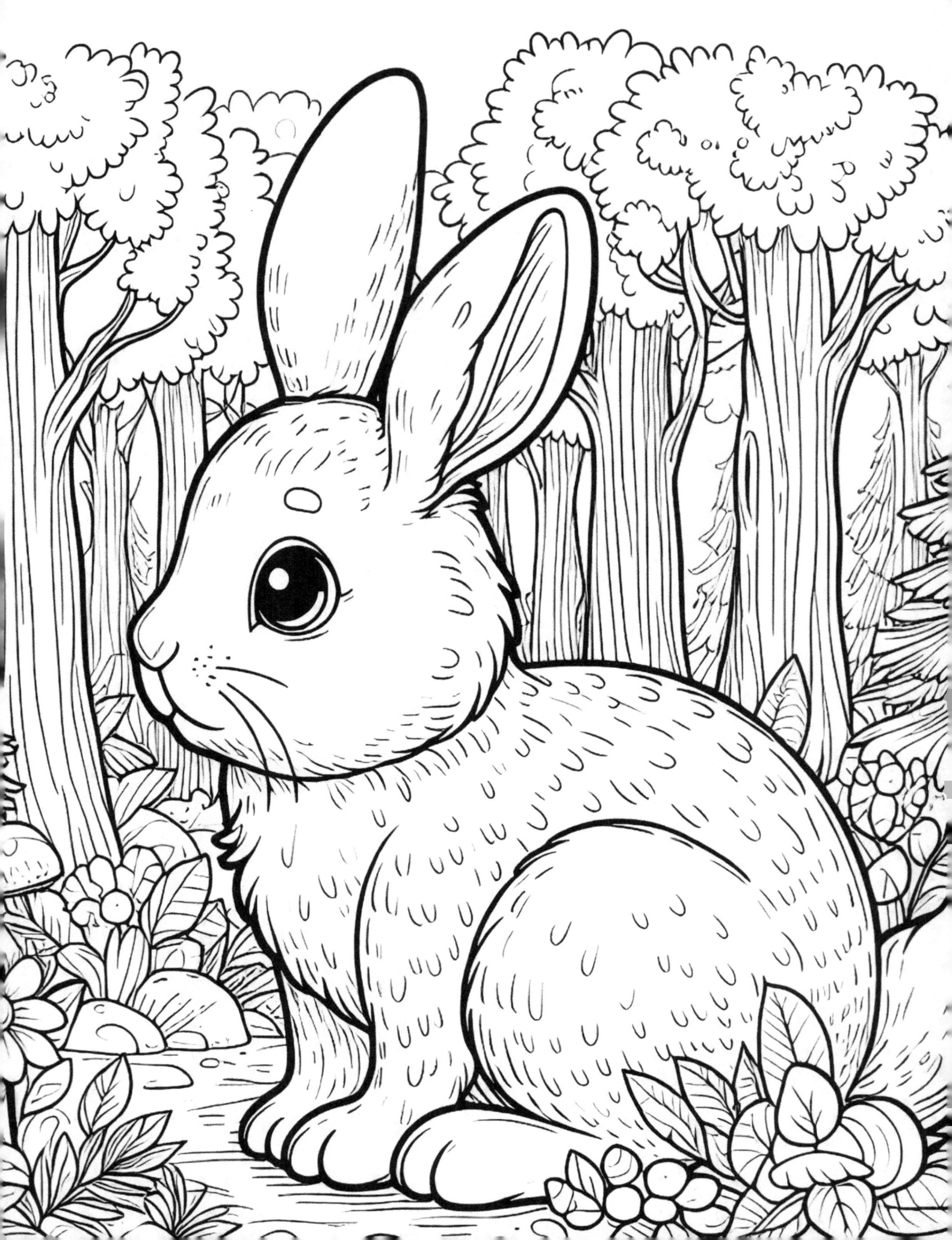

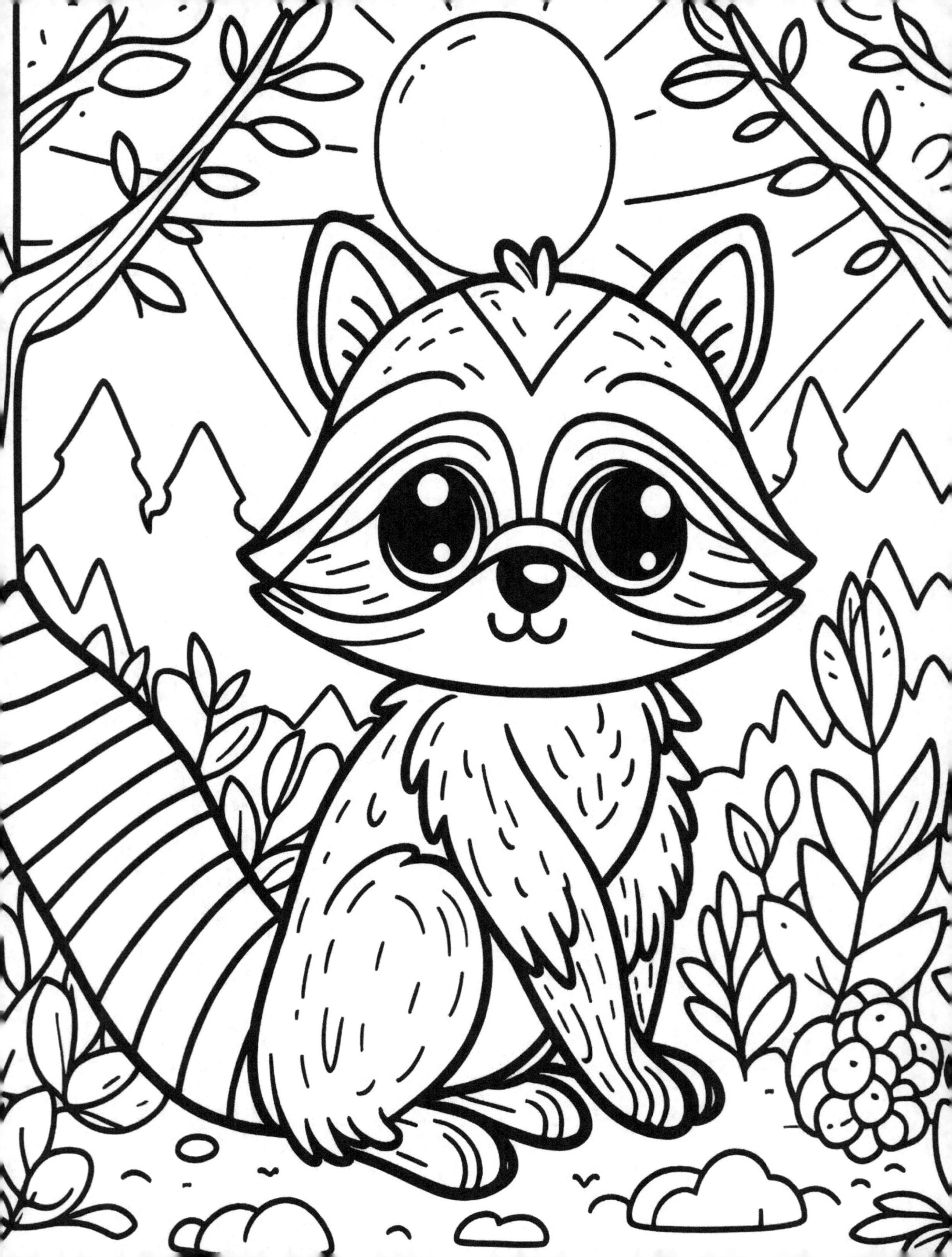

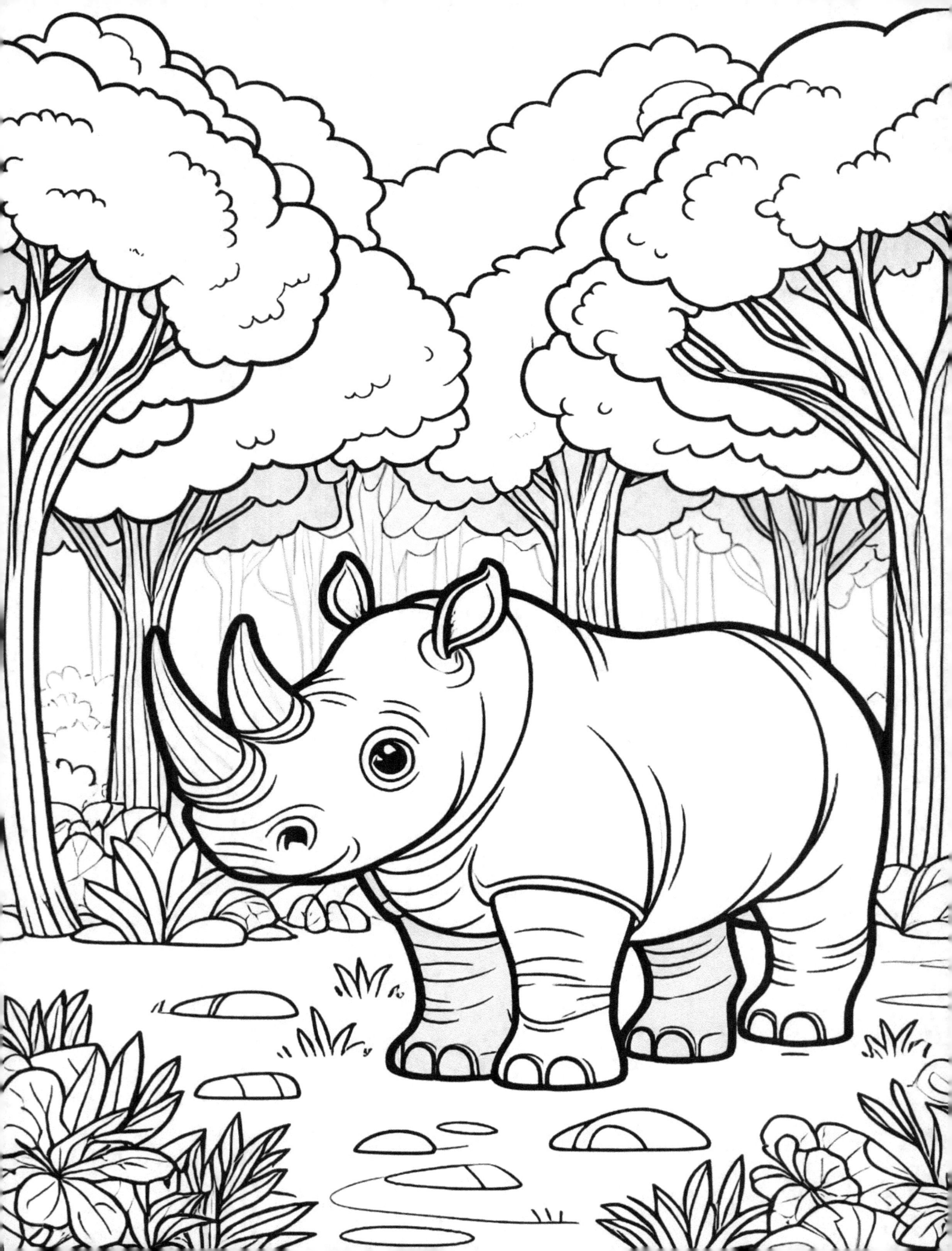

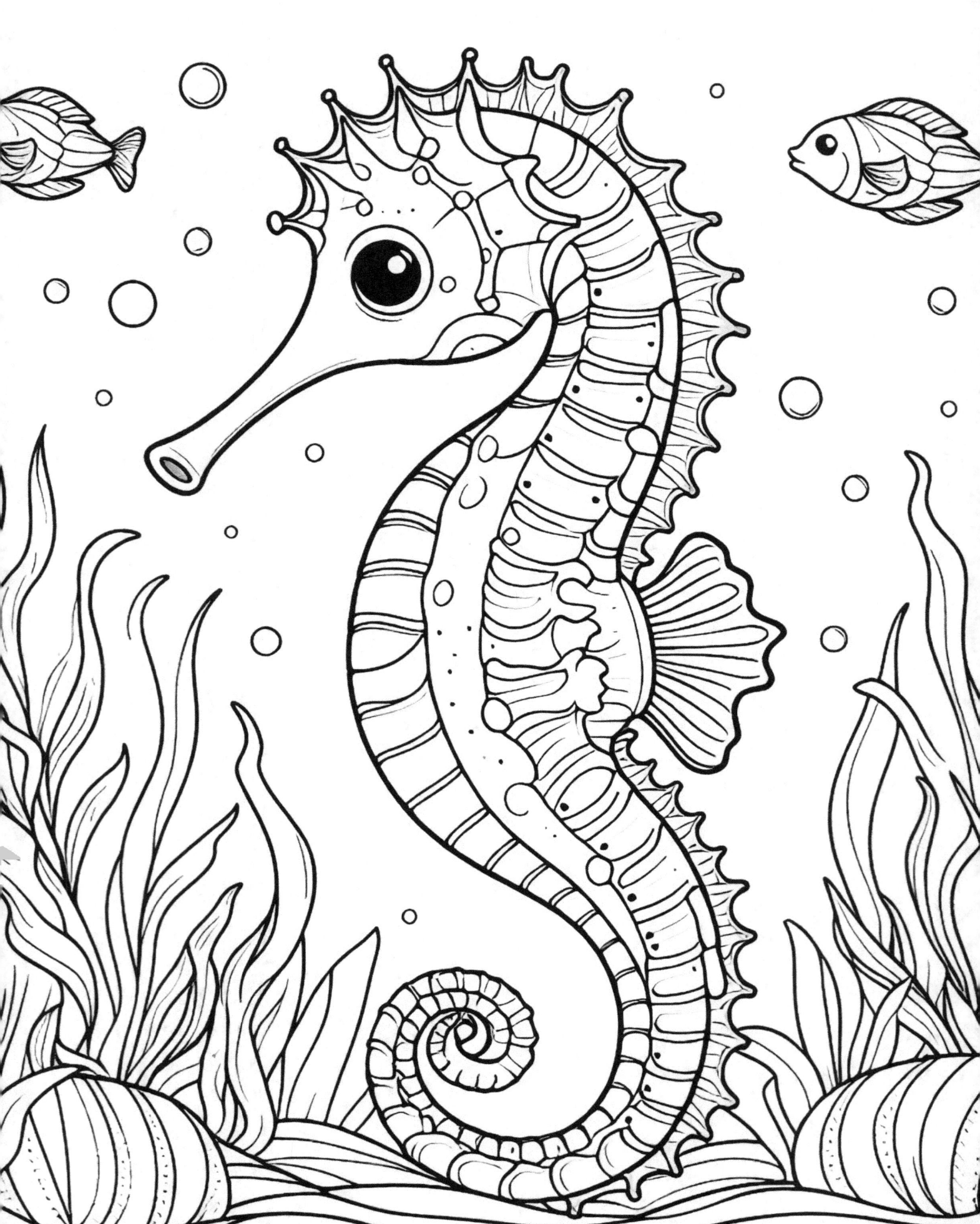

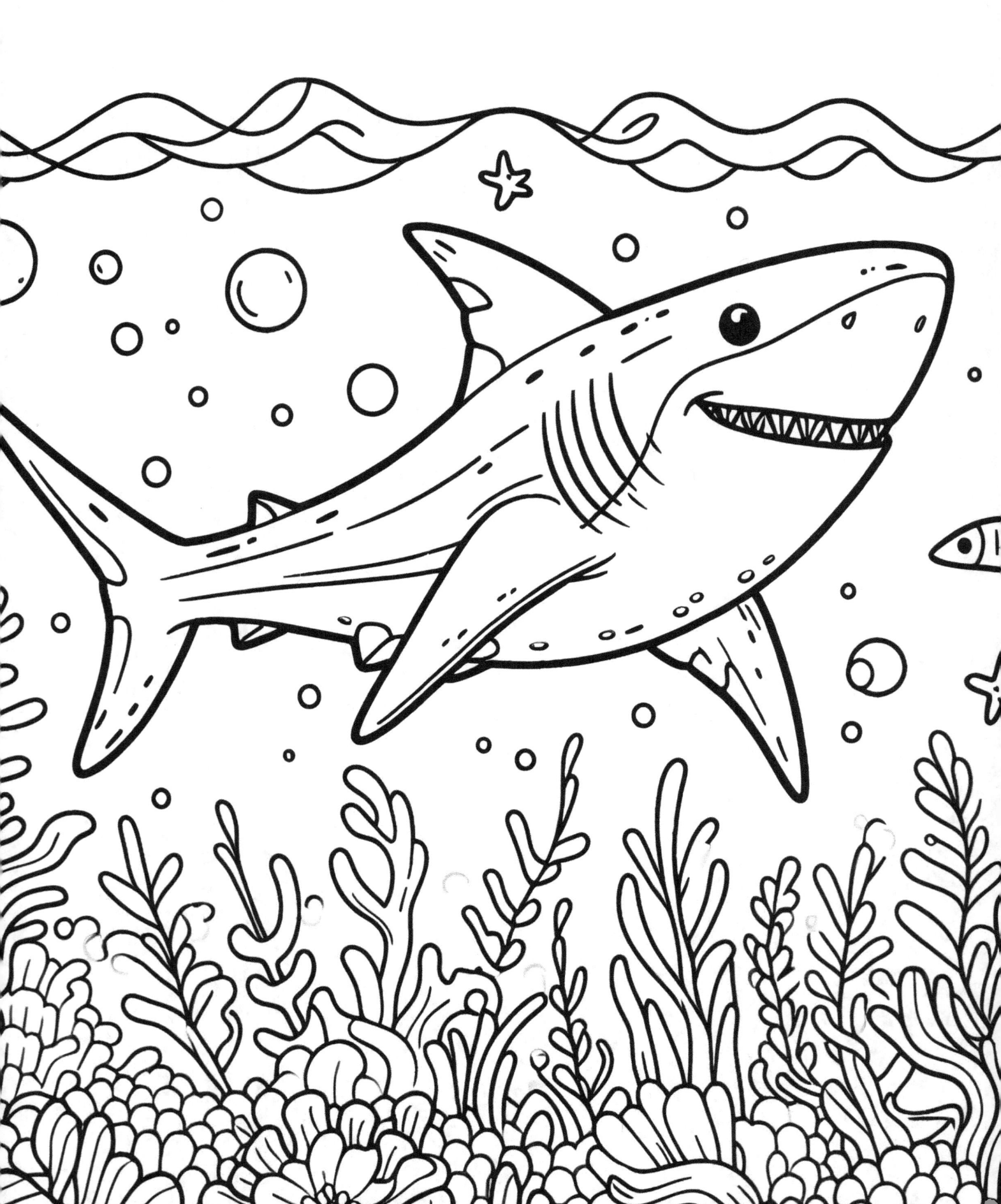

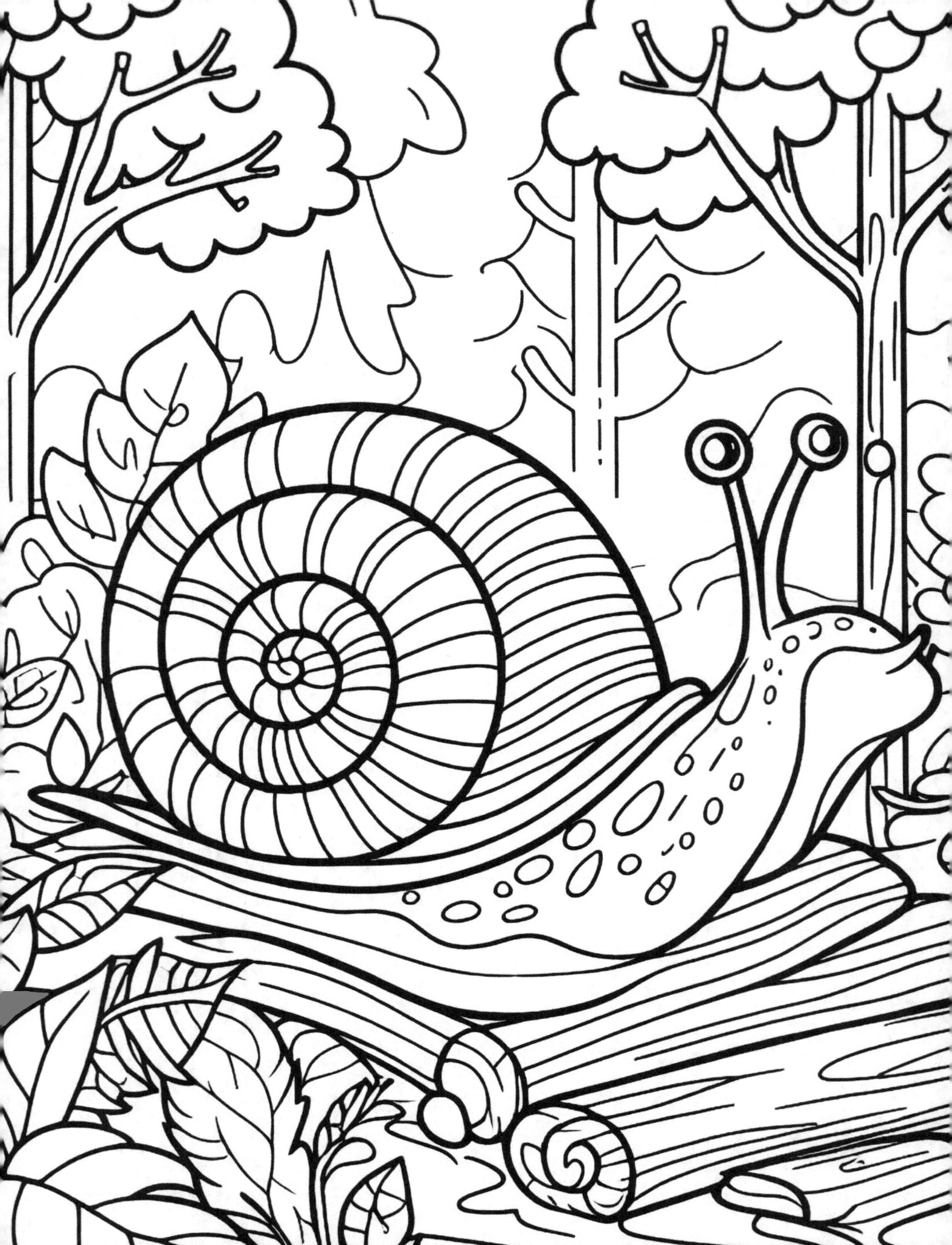

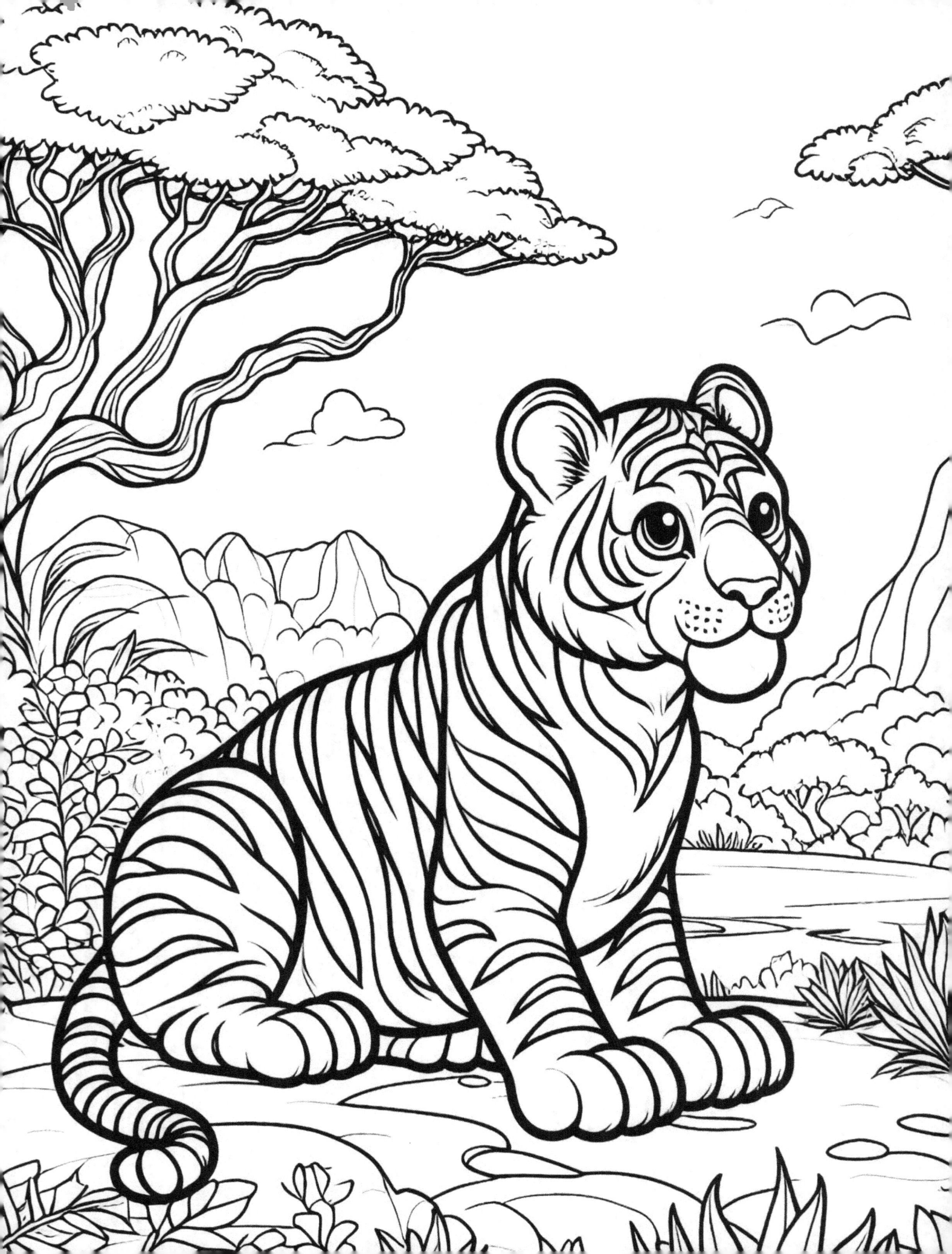

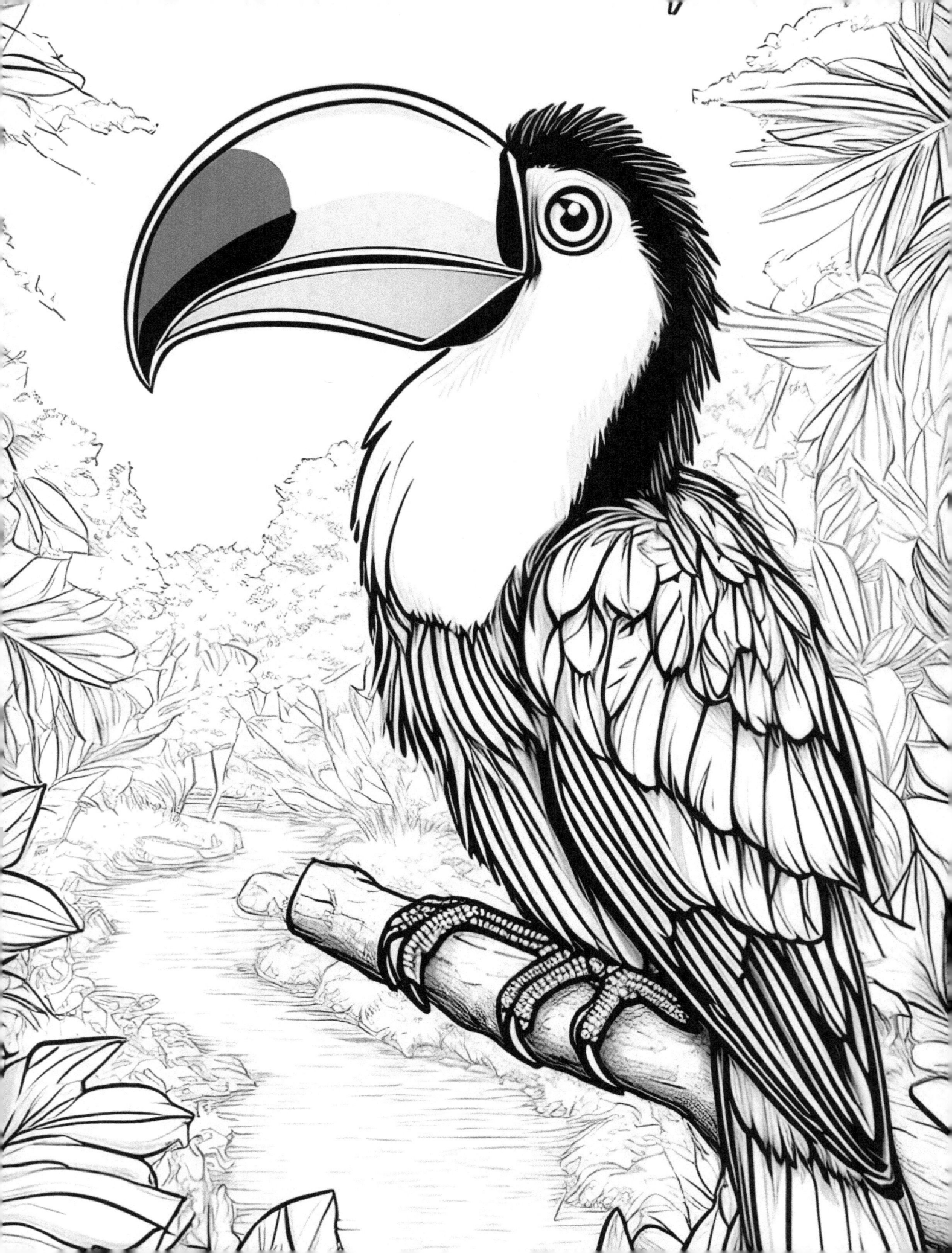

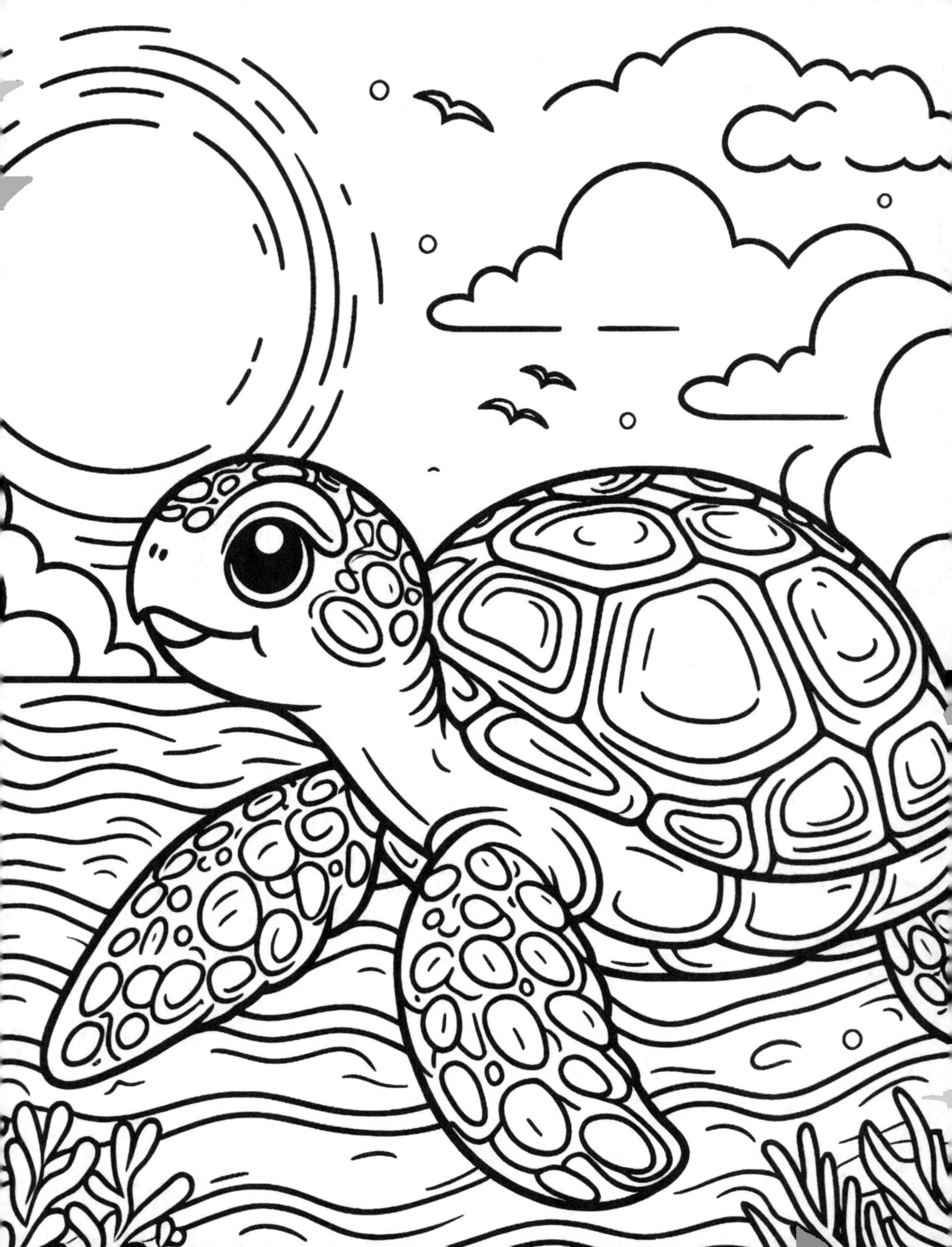

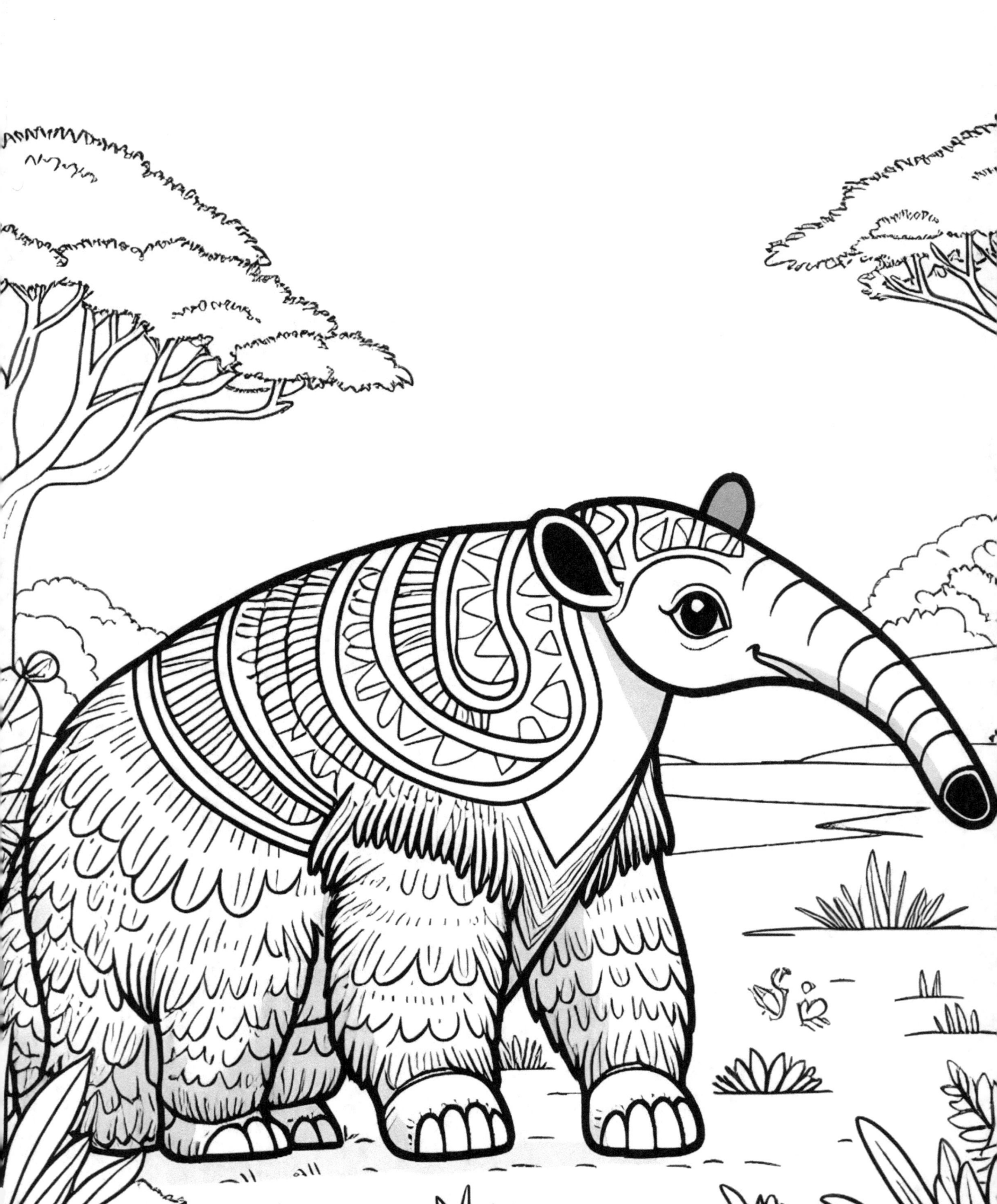

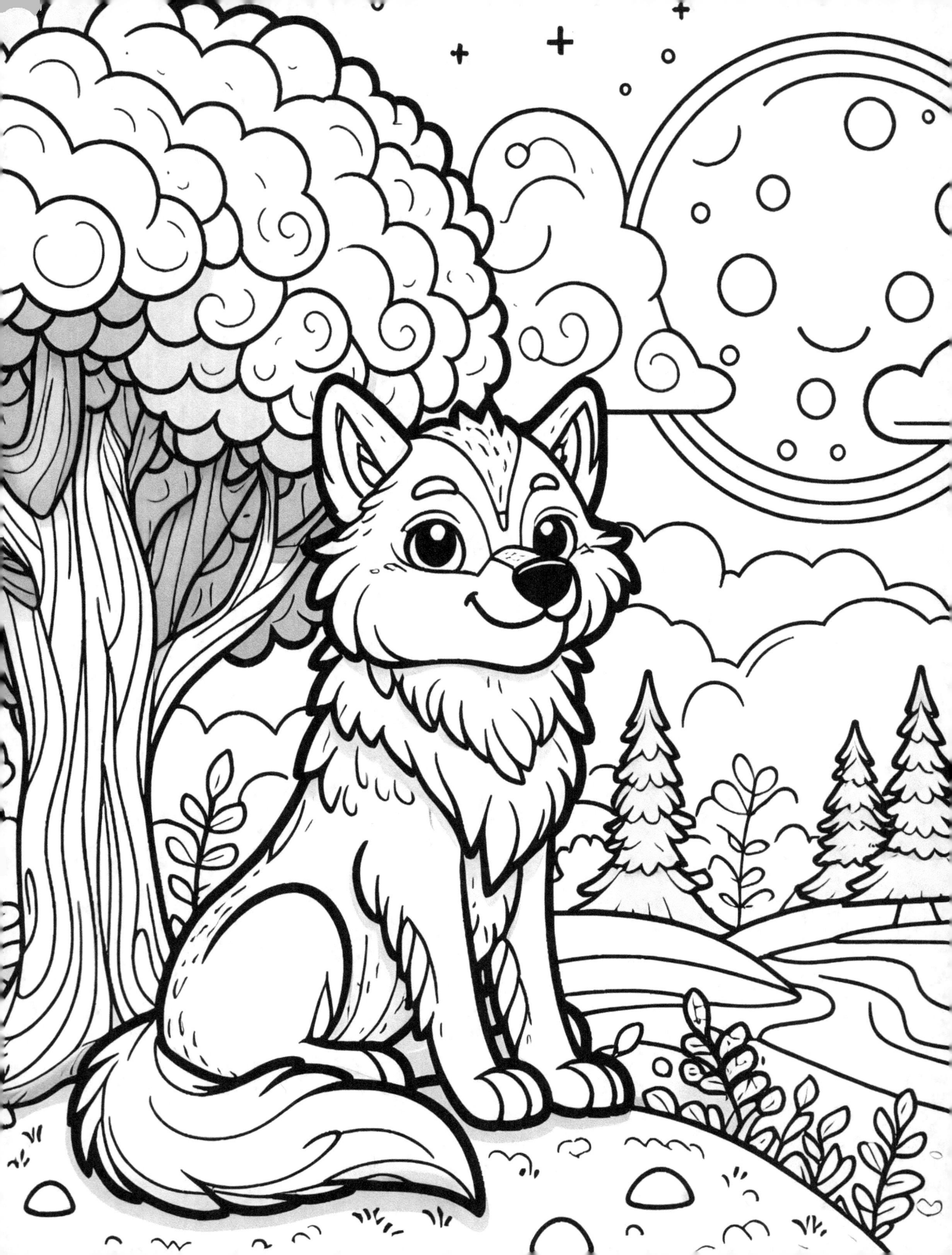

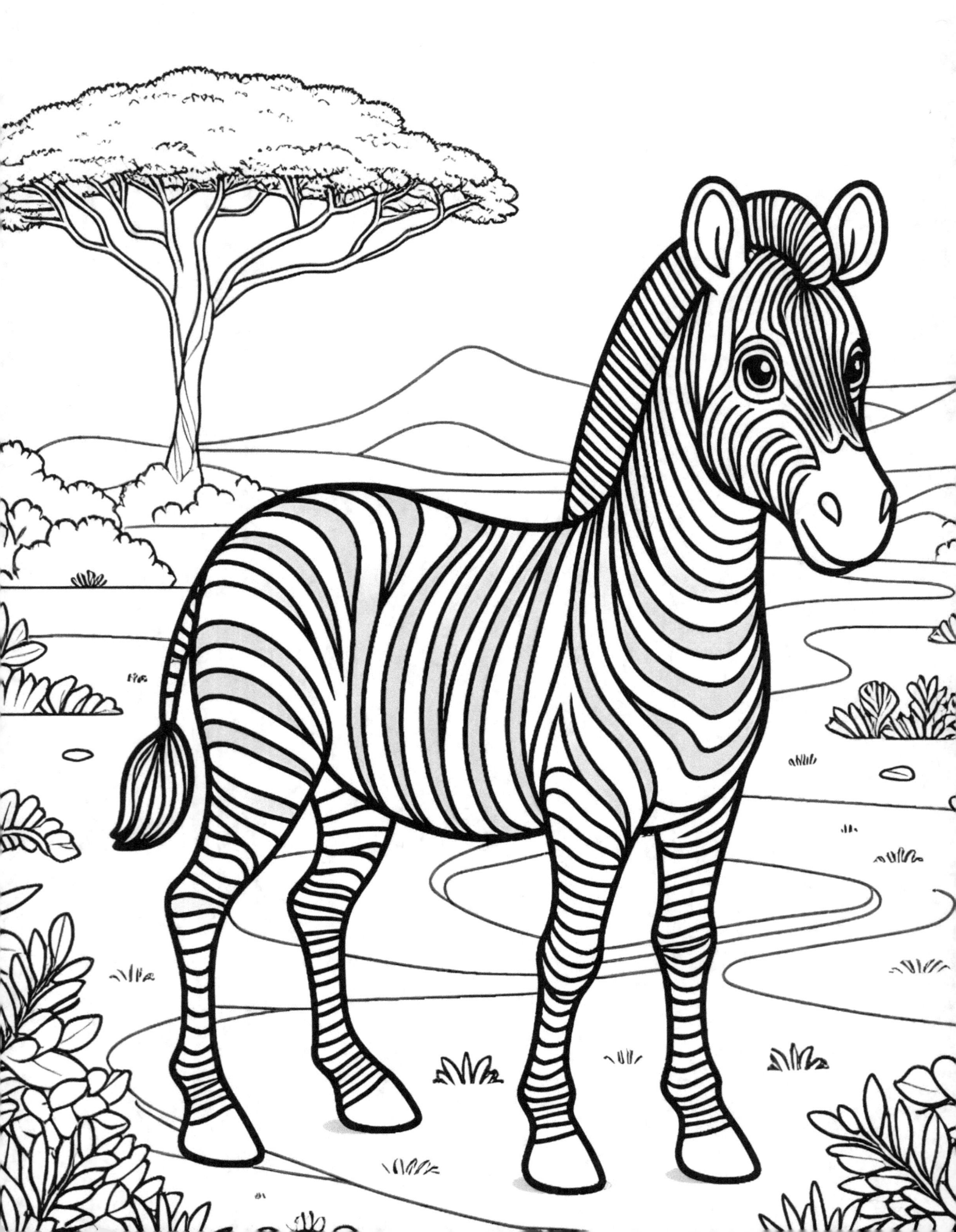